KNOWING

KNOWING THE FATHER'S HEART

KNOWING THE FATHER'S HEART

KNOWING THE FATHER'S HEART

KNOWING THE FATHER'S HEART

OTHER BOOKS BY ROBERT GARRETT
www.robertgarrett.org

CHRISTIAN CALL BIBLE INSTITUTE
www.christiancallbibleinstitute.com

- God's Covenant Love
- God's Unconditional Love
- Kerygma, Volume 1
- Kerygma, Volume 2
- Living the Blessed Life
- People of His Presence
- Suffering Servant of the LORD
- The Call to Authentic Discipleship
- The Triune Love of God
- The Wondrous Exchange
- Worship in Spirit and Truth

ROBERT GARRETT MINISTRIES
PO Box 238, Downingtown, PA 19335

KNOWING THE FATHER'S HEART

KNOWING THE FATHER'S HEART

Robert Garrett
© 2016

CCP | CHRISTIAN CALL PRESS

KNOWING THE FATHER'S HEART
Robert Garrett

Christian Call Bible Institute
PO Box 238, Downingtown, PA 19335
www.christiancallbibleinstitute.org

CCP | CHRISTIAN CALL PRESS

Christian Call Press and Christian Call Bible Institute are subsidiaries of Christian Call Inc. Christian Call ™ is a registered trademark

© 2016 by Christian Call, Inc.
Revised December 24, 2016
All rights reserved!

ISBN: 9781682737507

20 19 18 17 16 15 14 13 12 11 10 9 8 7 6 5 4 3

No part of this publication may be reproduced or transmitted in any form or by any means, electronic, or mechanical, including photocopy, recording or any information storage and retrieval system, without permission in writing from the author.

Printed in the United States of America

Some Scripture quotations taken from the King James Version. Cambridge University Press, University Printing House, Shaftesbury Road, Cambridge.

Some Scripture quotations taken from the New King James Version®. Copyright © 1982 by Thomas Nelson.

Some Scripture quotations taken from the New American Standard Bible®, Copyright © 1960, 1962, 1963, 1968, 1971, 1972, 1973, 1975, 1977, 1995 by The Lockman Foundation.

Some Scripture quotations taken from the New English Bible, copyright © Cambridge University Press and Oxford University Press 1961, 1970.

Some Scripture quotations taken from the New International Version ® NIV ® Copyright © 1973, 1978, 1984 by International Bible Society ®

The cover picture of this book is in the public domain.

TABLE OF CONTENTS

- Opening Texts; *Two Introductory Passages*
- General Introduction; *Preparing to Study*
- General Outline; *The Prodigal Son Parable*

Knowing the Father's Heart (Part-1)
THEOLOGICAL IMPLICATIONS OF LOVE

- Knowing God; *The Father Himself loves you* ....
- The Divine Imperative; *Rejoice with me* ....
- The Joy of the Lord; *Anticipating Grace* ....
- The Dance of God; *the Divine Perichoresis* ....
- Life is Dynamic Movement; *Consider the atom* ....
- Intimate Fellowship; *the closest relationship* ....
- Life in the Trinity; *forgotten heart of the faith* ....
- Face to Face with God; *Jesus our representative* ....
- His identity and ours; *so are we in this world* ....
- New Creation in Christ; *the one for the many* ....
- God's Essential Nature; *Unconditional Love* ....
- Through the Looking Glass; *the Jesus Model* ....
- Seven-fold Emptying; *the seven-downs* ....
- Seven-fold Exaltation; *the seven-ups* ....
- Love, Glory and Election; *Jesus is Lord of all* ....
- The Primary Doctrine; *Trinitarian Love* ....
- Monarchy of the Father; *Practical Implications* ....
- Identity and Destiny; *Life in the Spirit* ....
- Effects of the Fall; *Source of Significance* ....
- Study Questions (part-1) ....

Knowing the Father's Heart (Part-2)
PRACTICAL IMPLICATIONS OF LOVE

- A Parable is; *Earthly story, heavenly meaning* ....
- There was a Man; *God's heart in a metaphor* ....
- Father's apparent inaction; *Why God allows it* ....
- Jesus is God from God; *no God behind the back of Jesus* ....
- The Nicene Creed; *Universal confession of the church* ....
- Into a Far Country; *man's sad exile* ....
- O Happy Fault; *understanding The Fall* ....
- Lost but valuable; *intrinsic value in God's sight* ....
- Understanding love-wrath; *God is not bipolar* ....
- Love must be Free; *whosoever will may come* ....
- Good, Good Father; *shifting our understanding* ....
- Combating the Religious Spirit; *performance vs belonging*...
- Tale of Two Prodigals; *sinful prodigal, religious prodigal* ....
- God's Steadfast Mercy; *Covenant-love and loyalty* ....
- Conceptions of the Afterlife; *the lens of C.S. Lewis* ....
- Defining Personhood; *A being in relationship* ....
- The Running Father; *the pursuing love of God* ....
- The Bema Seat; *rewards won or lost* ....
- The Glorious Gospel; *the Good News* ....
- It is finished; *sin has been conquered* ....
- Avoiding Extremes; *caution on either side* ....
- Welcome home; *returning from self-imposed exile* ....
- Gracious Gifts of God; *the unworthy made worthy* ....
- Making it practical; *Why God's love is primary* ....
- Study Questions (part-2) ....
- Recommended Reading ....
- Partial Bibliography ....
- Endnotes ....

KNOWING THE FATHER'S HEART

OPENING TEXTS
(Two introductory passages)

And in that day, you will ask Me nothing. Most assuredly, I say to you, whatever you ask the Father in My Name He will give you. Until now you have asked nothing in My name. Ask, and you will receive, that your joy may be full. "These things I have spoken to you in figurative language; but the time is coming when I will no longer speak to you in figurative language, but I will tell you plainly about the Father. In that day, you will ask in My name, and I do not say to you that I shall pray the Father for you; <u>for the Father, Himself loves you</u>, because you have loved Me, and have believed that I came forth from God. I came forth from the Father and have come into the world. Again, I leave the world and go to the Father *(John 16:23-28 NKJV)*.

---

11 And he said, "There was a man who had two sons. 12 And the younger of them said to his father, 'Father, give me the share of property that is coming to me.' And he divided his property between them. 13 Not many days later, the younger son gathered all he had and took a journey into a far country, and there he squandered his property in reckless living. 14 And when he had spent everything, a severe famine arose in that country, and he began to be in need. 15 So he went and hired himself out to[a] one of the citizens of that country, who sent him into his fields to feed pigs. 16 And he was longing to be fed with the pods that the pigs ate, and no one gave him anything. 17 "But when he came to himself, he said, 'How many of my father's hired servants have more than enough bread, but I perish here with hunger! 18 I will

arise and go to my father, and I will say to him, "Father, I have sinned against heaven and before you. 19 I am no longer worthy to be called your son. Treat me as one of your hired servants.'" 20 And he arose and came to his father. But while he was still a long way off, his father saw him and felt compassion, and ran and embraced him and kissed him. 21 And the son said to him, 'Father, I have sinned against heaven and before you. I am no longer worthy to be called your son.' 22 But the father said to his servants, 'Bring quickly the best robe, and put it on him, and put a ring on his hand, and shoes on his feet. 23 And bring the fattened calf and kill it, and let us eat and celebrate. 24 For this my son was dead, and is alive again; he was lost, and is found.' And they began to celebrate. 25 "Now his older son was in the field, and as he came and drew near to the house, he heard music and dancing. 26 And he called one of the servants and asked what these things meant. 27 And he said to him, 'Your brother has come, and your father has killed the fattened calf, because he has received him back safe and sound.' 28 But he was angry and refused to go in. His father came out and entreated him, 29 but he answered his father, 'Look, these many years I have served you, and I never disobeyed your command, yet you never gave me a young goat, that I might celebrate with my friends. 30 But when this son of yours came, who has devoured your property with prostitutes, you killed the fattened calf for him!' 31 And he said to him, 'Son, you are always with me, and all that is mine is yours. 32 It was fitting to celebrate and be glad, for this your brother was dead, and is alive; he was lost, and is found'" (Luke 15 ESV).

GENERAL INTRODUCTION
(Preparing to study)

What you are holding is not a traditional textbook. Rather, you are reading a collection of graduate-level lecture notes prepared by the author; centered around The Prodigal Son Parable. Some portion of this material was originally presented *live* at Fisherman's Net Church in Venice, FL in the summer of 2016, and assumes a certain foundational, theological background. Furthermore, this publication is a student study-guide intended to supplement lectures presented at *Knowing the Father's Heart* seminars. For those taking this course through *Christian Call Bible Institute,* please refer to the current CCBI Student Handbook for more detail. Please also refer to the endnotes for additional commentary on related topics as well as general reference. The reader will notice many questions are asked throughout the study. This is because the material presented here is catechetical [1] in nature.

Let us now say a word about the audience to whom the Prodigal Son Parable of was originally spoken. We should take note of what immediately precedes the Parable of the Prodigal Son; namely, the Parable of the Lost Sheep and the Parable of the Lost Coin. In seeking to understand the latter, we must understand the whole. All three go together in some way and relate to the same theme; namely, a revelation of the heart of God. Furthermore, it is important to know not only *what* the parable means, but to *whom* it was spoken. Jesus' audience was the Scribes and Pharisees; who were complaining to Jesus that He associated/had table-fellowship with tax collectors and sinners (Luke 15:1-2), which was a great offense to the religious leaders of His day. But Jesus intentionally sat and eat with publicans and sinners (Mark 2:13-17) as well as Scribes and Pharisees (Luke 15:1-2). Jesus loves all mankind! "God is love"

(1 Jn. 4:8). It is our fervent prayer that our general readership come to know the unconditional love of the Father, the unmerited grace of the Son, and holy communion of the Spirit.

KNOWING GOD
(The Father Himself loves you!)

> *... In that day, you will ask in My name, and I do not say to you that I shall pray the Father for you; for the Father, Himself loves you, because you have loved Me, and have believed that I came forth from God...*

God said through the Old Testament prophet Malachi (1:2): *"'I have loved you,' says the Lord. 'Yet you say, in what way have You loved us?'"* Like the Israelites of old, sometimes we face the topic of God's unconditional love with a degree of doubt or suspicion. We ask such questions as... 'if God really loved me, then how come He didn't (apparently) answer this prayer or that prayer' (fill in the blank)? Our personal expectations are often not realized, which in turn, has a negative impact on the way some people view the love of God. Regardless, however, of the opinion that some people have towards God's love, the Holy Scriptures give us the true opinion we must have towards God's love. God says... *"I have loved you".* But we so often say... *"but how have you loved me"?* The short answer, and the most profound answer is – He has loved us IN CHRIST (through the incarnation, life, death, resurrection, ascension to God's right hand, and the gift of the Holy Spirit). We have amplified that point in the next section. Once we come to understand what God has already done for us in Christ, and the fact that what has been done for is complete (i.e. a past-tense reality: Jesus said, "it is finished"), then we can begin to walk in the blessings of God, presently, for we are already as blessed as we can be! The most important blessing of all is to know the truth: THE FATHER HIMSELF LOVES YOU!

> *Blessed be the God and Father of our Lord Jesus Christ, who has blessed us in Christ with every spiritual blessing in the heavenly places (Ephesians 1:3 ESV).*

How do we know the Father loves us? There are several reasons why the Father, Himself, loves us, as revealed in Holy Scripture:

1. Creation proves God's glory and nature (which is love).

> *The heavens declare the glory of God; the skies proclaim the work of his hands. Day after day they pour forth speech; night after night they display knowledge. There is no speech or language where their voice is not heard. Their voice goes out into all the earth, their words to the ends of the world" (Psalm 19:1-4).*

> *Ever since the creation of the world his eternal power and DIVINE NATURE, invisible though they are, have been understood and seen through the things he has made. So, they are without excuse" (Romans 1:20).*

2. The Incarnation and Atonement proves God's love.

> *In this the love of God was manifested toward us, that God has sent His only begotten Son into the world, that we might live through Him. IN THIS IS LOVE, not that we loved God, but that He loved us and sent His Son to be the propitiation for our sins (1 John 4:8-10).*

3. Belonging to the family of God proves God's love.

   Behold what manner of love the Father has bestowed on us, that we should be called children of God! (1 John 3:1).

With that background, let us consider the basic outline of the Prodigal Son Parable – since it is the primary framework for all the various subthemes presented in this book.

GENERAL OUTLINE [2]
(The Prodigal Son Parable)

1. **YOUNGER PRODIGAL: A HARSH REALITY (Lk. 15:11-12; Deut. 21:17)**

   a. A shocking request ("… give me the share of property that is coming to me…") (i.e. I wish you were dead!)

   b. A selfish request ("… give me…)

2. **YOUNGER PRODIGAL: A HARD REALITY (Lk. 15:13-16). We should be careful what we ask for – we might get it)**

   a. The reality of sin's pleasures (Lk. 15:13; Hebrews 11:35)

   b. The reality of sin's price

      i. Sin brings separation (… took a journey into a far country…) (spiritual death) (Isa. 59:2; Jer. 31:3, John 3:16)

      ii. Sin brings sorrow (… he began to be in want…) (Rom. 6:23; James 1:14-15; Gal. 6:9)

c. The reality of sin's pain
   i. Sin brings shame (1 John 2:28)
   ii. Sin brings suffering (Proverbs 13:15)
   iii. Sin brings sadness

3. **YOUNGER PRODIGAL: A HUMBLE REALITY** (Lk. 15:17-20a)

   a. The son's realization (...when he came to himself... v17)

   b. The son's resolve (makes up his mind to return home, regardless of motive)

4. **YOUNGER PRODIGAL: A HAPPY REUNION** (Lk. 15:20b-24)

   a. He found reception (verses 20-21)

      i. Father ran towards him: it was considered undignified for an elderly man to run in that culture. So why did he do it? (Deut. 21:18-21). God runs to meet the sinner to quickly extend mercy and put away the danger! The father literally interposes Himself between the wrath of the village and the son, so that if the neighbors cast stones (it would have been common in this circumstance), they would have struck the father first (see Romans 8:33-34)

      ii. Father kissed him: (Gr: in the present-tense: i.e. "continual kissing"). The ultimate sign of acceptance. The prodigal son found love, forgiveness and reconciliation, instead of judgment and death (a feast instead of a funeral)

    iii. Father gifted him

        1. The best robe
        2. Ring on his hand
        3. Shoes on his feet
        4. Threw him a party

5. **ELDER PRODIGAL: HIS RESPECTABILITY** (verse 25a)

    a. He was a leader. As the 'elder-brother', he was entitled to two-thirds of His father's possessions (Deut. 21:17). Since his younger brother has already received his part of the inheritance (v12), everything belongs to this brother. When his father dies, not only will he receive his father's possessions, he will also become the legal and religious head of the family. Much has been given to this young man already, and more is on the way. He was already blessed!

    b. He was a laborer. When we first meet this man, he is "in the fields". He is busy doing his father's business (while his younger brother has been off in the far country wasting his father's inheritance). This man, had been working hard. And it appears that all is well in this family, and that there is good fellowship between the father and this older boy. This elder son is the picture of the religious elite.

6. **ELDER PRODIGAL: HIS RESENTMENT** (verse 25b-30). When he hears this, he becomes "angry." The word means "to become red-faced." It speaks of a person clenching their fists, and becoming red with anger. In his actions, here, his

resentment toward the father and His brother can be clearly seen.

   a. He did not love his father
   b. He did not love his younger brother
   c. His resentment is seen in his motives (verse 29)

      i. He did not care that his lost brother had come home
      ii. He did not care about what pleased the father
      iii. He saw his service to the father as slavery (v29) ("all these years I have been in bondage to you"). This is also seen in many church-goers

   d. His resentment is seen in his mentality (verse 30; Mt. 15:18-19)

   e. His resentment is seen in his methods

      i. It was a sign of disrespect to fail to greet one's father with a proper title. Even the younger brother did this (v12)
      ii. It was disrespectful for the elder-son to argue with his father, which he did in front of the servants and the guests. He brought as much, or maybe more, disgrace upon the father as the younger son, because he did what he did in public

7. ELDER PRODIGAL: HIS REACTION (verses 28, 31-32)

   a. He refused the father's plea. The father went out and "entreated" this boy to come in to the feast. The word "entreat" means "to come alongside of another to offer aid and comfort, to beg, to console, to comfort, to encourage." It is the same word that is translated "Comforter" in John 16:13

b. **He refused the father's promises.** The father praised him for his efforts, and reminded him that everything was already his! In effect, this father was saying, "I value you and our relationship far more than I value your works." This boy could have enjoyed fellowship with the father anytime he wanted, but apparently, he was too wrapped up in his own legalism and narrow-mindedness to realize it.

c. **He refused the father's passion.** The father tells this boy that is was "meet" that they should have this celebration. The word "meet" means "necessary". To the father, the return of the lost son was a cause for celebration. The Father was passionate about the younger son's return. A lost one had been found. One considered dead was now alive again. And, most importantly, a father's love and faith had been vindicated and the family name restored. Everyone is happy but the elder brother. Bottom line: every individual must write his or her own ending to this story!" [3]

~ *Knowing the Father's Heart (Part 1)* ~
THEOLOGICAL IMPLICATIONS OF LOVE

THE DIVINE IMPERATIVE:
(Rejoice with me!)

    The prodigal son parable is so famous that we might be tempted to think it needs no introduction much less an extended commentary. No doubt this parable has inspired countless preachers, teachers, artists and writers over the centuries. We may remember Rembrandt's famous painting with the younger son on his knees before the forgiving father. That painting has become nearly as inspirational as the parable itself. Overall, it is obvious both from the painting and the story itself that God is gracious and loving; ready to forgive and eager to restore the penitent. This is the heart of God and the overriding theme of our present study.

> Rembrandt's final word is given in his monumental painting. Here he interprets the Christian idea of mercy with an extraordinary solemnity, as though this were his spiritual testament to the world. The father and the Prodigal Son stand out in light against an enormous dark surface. Particularly vivid are the ragged garment of the

son, and the old man's sleeves, which are ochre tinged with golden olive; the ochre color combined with an intense scarlet red in the father's cloak forms an unforgettable coloristic harmony. The son, ruined and repellent, with his bald head and the appearance of an outcast, returns to his father's house after long wanderings and many vicissitudes. He has wasted his heritage in foreign lands and has sunk to the condition of a swineherd. His old father, dressed in rich garments, as are the assistant figures, has hurried to meet him before the door and receives the long-lost son with the utmost fatherly-love. [5]

6

The Return of the Prodigal Son is an oil painting by Rembrandt. It is among the Dutch master's final works, likely completed within two years of his death in 1669.

Phrases from this famed parable like: *"bring hither the fatted calf, and kill it; and let us eat, and be merry,"* as stated in the King James version, have become renowned and are essential to our understanding of God's father heart. This phrase speaks of the heavenly Father's desire. We might even call it, the divine imperative: *Let us eat and be merry!* This imperative/command reminds us that the center of worship for Christians is indeed, the meal of covenant; *the Eucharist.* The word Eucharist means: *The Great Thanksgiving.* Throughout most of church history, the Communion Table (not the Altar Call) [7] is central in public liturgy; representing the pinnacle of worship. The parable of the prodigal son shows us this truth in metaphor. Corporate fellowship and prayer, together with Word and Sacrament is that which fully reveals Christ to our hearts; opening the inside eyes of our understanding that we might "know Him."

> When he was at the table with them, he took bread, gave thanks, broke it and began to give it to them. Then their eyes were opened and they recognized him, and he disappeared from their sight. They asked each other, "Were not our hearts burning within us while he talked with us on the road and opened the Scriptures to us? (Luke 24:30-32 NIV).
>
> They devoted themselves to the apostles' teaching and to fellowship, to the breaking of bread and to prayer (Acts 2:42 NIV).

When Holy Communion is properly celebrated in all its mystery and majesty, the atoning sacrifice of Christ is revealed, which communicates the unconditional love of God. There is a beauty in the Gospel like none other; when properly understood, and presented. "How beautiful on the mountains are the feet of those who bring good news, who proclaim peace, who bring good tidings, who proclaim salvation, who say to Zion, 'Your God reigns!'" (Isa. 52:7)). Speaking of how beautiful the Gospel is – when properly witnessed... consider the testimony of the Russian Ambassadors in 987AD when they reported back to Prince Vladimir of Kiev about the Christianity they witnessed in Constantinople, which became the impetus for the eventual Christianization of Russia more than a millennium ago:

> We knew not whether we were in heaven or on earth, for surely there is no such splendor or beauty anywhere on earth. We cannot describe it to you; we only know that God dwells there among men and that their Service surpasses the worship of all other places... [8]

In the parable of the prodigal son, Holy Communion was indeed the father's imperative. The parable affirms this. Notice how the father ignored the prodigal's ridiculous comments about no longer deserving to be a son. Notice that the father refused to acknowledge his lost son's "orphan spirit" and immediately set out to restore him with the climatic phrase: *"let us eat and be merry."* This command has cosmic implications and reveals the ultimate plan of God for all redeemed mankind. It speaks of the feast of the New Covenant church which celebrates Christ's finished work on Calvary. We see this truth expressed in the book of Revelation at the Marriage Supper of the Lamb; which is another way of describing the centrality of Holy Communion in the life of the church, both in this age and thereafter. The greatest calling of the church is to the Lord's table. It is the highest privilege of all.

> Then I heard what seemed to be the voice of a great multitude, like the roar of many waters and like the sound of mighty peals of thunder, crying out, "Hallelujah! For the Lord our God the Almighty reigns. Let us rejoice and exult and give him the glory, for the

marriage of the Lamb has come, and his Bride has made herself ready; it was granted her to clothe herself with fine linen, bright and pure"— for the fine linen is the righteous deeds of the saints. And the angel said to me, "Write this: Blessed are those who are invited to the marriage supper of the Lamb." And he said to me, "These are the true words of God". (Rev. 19:6-9 ESV).

In this present life, people the world over generally agree that the preferred place of meeting is around the kitchen table. Why is this? I believe it is the innate knowing of all people that there is something unique about the common meal. How much more, the *uncommon* meal (The Eucharist)? I think my favorite icon is the *Troitsa Holy Trinity* [9] which depicts the trinity seated at the communion table of fellowship.

[10]

The parable of the prodigal son is not merely about repentance and forgiveness (although it is about that initially). The parable is ultimately about restored fellowship and communion. The communion table reminds us that the work of redemption has been completed at Calvary. The revelation of this saving truth almost cries out: celebrate! Give thanks! The word Eucharist means: "The Great Thanksgiving." We are ever thankful about our forgiveness, our acceptance, our salvation, our new life in Christ. The Eucharist (the Lord's Supper) is about our inclusion in the Body of Christ. It is the meal of covenant communion. It is all about WHO WE ARE "IN CHRIST." The preposition: "in Christ" [11] is a master key in understanding the New Testament, and is perhaps the central theological theme in the writings of the Apostle Paul. If we fail to grasp this important truth, we likewise fail to understand a primary component in the New Covenant. Albert Schweitzer called "being-in-Christ" the prime enigma of Paul's teaching.

> For him [Paul], believers are redeemed by entering already, through the union with Christ, by means of a mystical dying and rising again with him during the continuance of the natural world-era into a supernatural state of existence, this state being that which they are to possess in the kingdom of God. Through Christ we are removed out of this world and transferred into the state of existence proper to the kingdom of God, notwithstanding the fact that it has not yet appeared. [12]

Consider the word phrases that Paul uses, for example, in Ephesians 1, to describe present-tense realities based upon the past-tense work of Calvary. Below are a few examples:

> (3) Blessed be the God and Father of our Lord Jesus Christ, who has blessed us in Christ with every spiritual blessing in the heavenly places, (4) even as <u>he chose us</u> in

him before the foundation of the world, that we should be holy and blameless before him. In love (5) he predestined us for adoption as sons through Jesus Christ, according to the purpose of his will, (6) to the praise of his glorious grace, with which <u>he has blessed us</u> in the Beloved. (7) In him we have redemption through his blood, the forgiveness of our trespasses, according to the riches of his grace, (8) which <u>he lavished</u> upon us, in all wisdom and insight (9) <u>making known</u> to us the mystery of his will, according to his purpose, which he set forth in Christ (10) as a plan for the fullness of time, to unite all things in him, things in heaven and things on earth. (11) In him <u>we have obtained</u> an inheritance, having been predestined according to the purpose of him who works all things according to the counsel of his will. (Ephesians 1:3-11 ESV).

To be more technical here: each of the five underlined phrases in Greek are in the *Aorist* tense and *Indicative* mood, which means that a simple action has occurred in the past. In Greek (the language of the New Testament), the only place where 'time' comes to bear directly upon the tense of a verb is the indicative mood. This means that the action is done; already accomplished. We have provided a chart in the endnotes which summaries this kind of action shown by each Greek verb tense with its corresponding time of action in the indicative mood. [13]

1. "He chose us in him before the foundation of the world" – *a past tense reality!*
2. "He has blessed us in the Beloved" – *a past tense reality!*
3. "He lavished upon us in all wisdom and insight" – *a past tense reality!*
4. "Making known to us the mystery of his will" – *a past tense reality!*

5. "We have obtained an inheritance, having been predestined according to His purpose" – *a past tense reality!*

The above passages reveal past tense realities... and this is only a partial list. The point here is that we are already as blessed as we can be "in Christ." This is true because of the finished work of Calvary. Fundamentally, our faith looks back! Present faith does not make it so... present faith simply receives it as so. The reality is true before we fully understood it or receive it. The victory is already ours "in Christ." To use the words of Christ on the cross: IT IS DONE. Of course, we must believe it and receive it to let it be. But our faith doesn't make it so; our faith merely releases it to us. We must simply claim and walk in the truth of the Gospel by the power of the indwelling Holy Spirit.

This all harkens back to the divine imperative of the father in the parable: *"rejoice with me."* Not only does the parable focus on the communion table, but it focuses on the celebration and dance that accompanies this feast. Why? Because full-provision has already been made. Now, let us celebrate! This reminds us that God likes to throw parties (in a holy kind of way, of course). We see this image presented in Luke chapter fifteen. It is the dance of the Lord. Consider the language: *"Let us eat and be merry."* The verb: *"let us make merry"* in Greek [14] conveys the idea of *cheer and merriment which is accompanied by an inner sense of triumph and victory.* We can call it the Lord's victory dance; the dance of triumph. Notice that the father's dance becomes our dance (the dance of the family) because we are "in Christ."

> But thanks, be to God, who in Christ always leads us in triumphal procession, and through us spreads the

fragrance of the knowledge of him everywhere (2 Corinthians 2:14 ESV).

The trio of parables in Luke fifteen repeat this idea each time for precisely this reason. It is an obviously repeated theme.

- Parable of the Lost Sheep (Luke 15:1-7) ends with the <u>Divine imperative</u>: *"Rejoice with me, for I have found my sheep that was lost" (verse 6). "Just so, I tell you, there will be more joy in heaven over one sinner who repents than over ninety-nine righteous persons who need no repentance" (verse 7).*

- Parable of the Lost Coin (Luke 15:8-10) ends with the same <u>Divine imperative</u>: *"Rejoice with me, for I have found the coin that I had lost" (verse 9). "Just so, I tell you, there is joy before the angels of God over one sinner who repents" (verse 10).*

- Parable of the Lost Son (Prodigal Son) (Luke 15:11-32) ends with the same <u>Divine imperative</u>, except greatly amplified: *"Bring quickly the best robe, and put it on him, and put a ring on his hand, and shoes on his feet" (verse 22). "Bring the fattened calf and kill it, and let us eat and celebrate" (verse 23). "For this my son was dead, and is alive again; he was lost, and is found.' And they began to celebrate" (verse 24). "Now his older son was in the field, and as he came and drew near to the house, he heard music and dancing" (verse 25). "... you never gave me a young goat, that I might celebrate with my friends"* (the accusation of the elder brother) *(verse 29). "It was fitting to celebrate and be glad, for this your brother was dead, and is alive; he was lost, and is found"* (the response of the father) *(verse 32).*

The whole tenor and purpose of this trio of parables in Luke fifteen is centered around, as we have said, not merely repentance and forgiveness, but ultimately, restored fellowship, dancing and celebration. In the Jewish culture, this sort of thing was commonplace. Jesus ends each parable with a command to join in the gladness and joy. This reveals the Divine motivation. Joy and celebration is the Divine imperative! I remember the first time we went to Israel on a tour in the year 1981 during the Christian celebration of the Feast of Tabernacles. I was only 18-years old at the time and overwhelmed by such a joyful expression as we joined with thousands and thousands dancing in the streets of Jerusalem; giving high praises unto God. I shall never forget it as long as I live! Our God is a dancing God! This is not an irreverent thing to say (as religion might call it; as the Elder Brother described it), but rather the opposite. It is the nature of God to be glad and rejoice.

15

We should allow this glorious truth to penetrate deep into our soul. God rejoices over even one lost sinner coming home! Why, we might ask? The answer is that God is unconditional love! This is His eternal nature. This is why God created us! We were created *for love* and *by love!* It is the father's heart to enjoy His people – and that we might enjoy His fellowship. *"Let us rejoice and be merry!"* This is what life is all about. Redeemed life in Christ is not supposed to be a static, an idle affair. Redeemed life in Christ is supposed to be with joy unspeakable and full of glory! The word "unspeakable" is an awesome word meaning: "unable to find expression in words." *"Whom having not seen, ye love; in whom, though now ye see him not, yet believing, ye rejoice with joy unspeakable and full of glory" (1 Peter 1:8 KJV).*

THE JOY OF THE LORD:
(Anticipating Grace)

The steps of a good man are ordered by the LORD, And He delights [takes pleasure in] in his way. (Psalm 37:23)

As a handful of sand thrown into the ocean, so are the sins of all flesh as compared with the mind of God. Just as a strongly flowing fountain is not blocked up by a handful of earth, so the compassion of the Creator is not overcome by the wickedness of his creatures. ~ (St. Isaac The Syrian) [16]

God's love is always linked with His joy... "But the fruit of the Spirit is love, joy, peace, forbearance, kindness, goodness, faithfulness, gentleness and self-control. Against such things there is no law. (Galatians 5:22-23 NKJV). Notice that the fruit of the Spirit (in the above text) is singular (not plural). That is because all fruit are in reality; expressions of the singular fruit of LOVE – of which the first expression is JOY. Joy (Gr. χαρά, *chara*) means: gladness, favor, the awareness of God's grace. To live in joy is to live in the awareness of God's favor! It doesn't mean everything is perfect on the outside, it just means that God is working all things out for our good and His eternal glory!

That's what joy does! Joy believes God; that His favor is enough to get us over whatever we are facing today! Joy is anticipating the abundant grace of God; which is enough in every situation of life! Joy is the overflow of the fullness of God's love. The Scriptures tells us that Jesus was anointed with the oil of joy above His fellows. Jesus was the most joyful human being that ever lived! He is the ultimate manifestation of joy; the very incarnation of joy unspeakable and full of glory. Jesus came into this world to make *His joy* into *our joy*. Jesus said: *"that my joy might remain in you" (John 15:11)*. This was (and is) the desire of God for all His children. The Christian life was never meant to be an endurance contest. The New Testament is replete with such language as "more than conquerors" (Romans 8:37) and "triumphant in Christ" (2 Corinthians 2:14) and so forth. Our joy does not guarantee an easy life, rather, our joy is the result despite all these things (all the trials of this present life). WE WIN through Him who loves us so! (Romans 8:37).

17

KNOWING THE FATHER'S HEART

God loves us because of WHO HE IS; GOD IS LOVE. This is so, not for anything lovely within us, but because God rejoices over us because of His internal nature. God is love! God is joy! God is peace! Etc.... God IS what He DOES. Whatever God *does* is because that is who He *is!* God's love and God's joy are not reactions to us (to our behavior). Rather, God's love and joy are manifestations of His own internal, immutable nature. We are often unlovely; disobedient and rebellious, and of course God doesn't love our sin, but God loves us unconditionally because of His unchanging nature. "God is love" (1 John 4:8). 7th century Syriac bishop; St. Isaac said, *"Our compassionate Creator is not overcome by the wickedness of His creatures."* Our wickedness does not influence God's unchanging nature. Sin didn't cause God to become gracious. God has always been gracious because God is love before time and creation. Furthermore, to say: God is love, automatically implies that God is relationship; from before creation. God did not need to create man to find fellowship. God is fellowship from eternity. God created mankind to share fellowship, not to find it! God is not a lonely monad; as the Muslim conception of God portrays.

The Koran says, *"Say not 'Trinity': desist: it will be better for you: for Allah is One God: glory be to Him: (far Exalted is He) above having a son"* (4:171). This is a blatantly false notion! The Bible correctly teaches that God is a tri-personal being, which means that God is relationship. Love requires fellowship; relationship with "others." I remember the first time I heard a preacher said, "I'm not single, I'm in relationship with God." I thought to myself, YES! That's it! That's the revelation! As Believers in Christ, we are never single; never solitary persons. Even if we were deserted on a desert island somewhere, we would still be in relationship! Why? Because we are never alone (Hebrews 13:5). I believe this revelation is the reason for the Believer's "new name" written down in glory (Revelation 2:17). Even our new-name has been hyphenated. We have an "in

Christ" hyphenated name now. In the tradition of the early church, to be baptized into Christ is to receive a Christian name (a renaming occurs). Jesus Himself experienced this in His baptism in the Jordan River (Matthew 3:17). To be perfectly clear about this – my "new name" in Christ, my Christian name is: *"Robert Garrett-Christ"*. We live a hyphenated life now! We are no longer our own. We have been bought with a price (1 Corinthians 6:20). At first glance, I know this sort of thinking may appear sacrilegious, almost blasphemous to some people. But never has a more important truth ever been told!! Jesus said, "You may ask me for anything in my name, and I will do it" (John 14:14). Only a person in relationship can talk like that! "Your life and mine is hidden with Christ in God" (Colossians 3:3). This truth reveals the reality of life itself. Love and relationship describes WHO God is! The life of God is the love of God; a love-life that is not static (as we have already stated), but dynamic and ever-moving. It is a Divine dance; three persons in dynamic orbit about each other, a dance of love, delight and adoration. This is who God is and has always been. He dances over us.

> *The LORD your God is with you, the Mighty Warrior who saves. He will take great delight in you; in his love, he will no longer rebuke you, but will rejoice over you with singing* (Zephaniah 3:17 NIV). *As a young man marries a young woman, so will your Builder marry you; as a bridegroom rejoices over his bride, so will your God rejoice over you (Isaiah 62:5 NIV).* We are solemnly warned by 'profound thinkers' not to let the shadow of our emotions fall upon God. No doubt there is a real danger there; but there is a worse danger; that of conceiving of a God who has no life and heart – and it is better to hold fast by this – that in Him is that which corresponds to what in us is gladness. We are often told, too, that the Jehovah of the Old Testament is a stern and repellent God, and the

religion of the Old Testament is gloomy and servile. But such a misconception is hard to maintain in the face of such words as these. [18]

THE DANCE OF GOD
(The Divine Perichoresis)

[19]

God is not a bookkeeper or an old professor or some kind of divine black hole who is so angst-ridden, so lonely and bored and needy he sucks the life out of everything around him. God exists as a triune relationship–Father, Son and Spirit. And it is not a dead or empty relationship. The Father, Son and Spirit are not like three bronze statues in the park–speechless, motionless, heartless. The Father likes His Son. He loves him, is absolutely thrilled with him, bursting with pride over him (Matthew 3:17; 17:5 and John 5:19-20). And the Son adores his Father, loves Him with all of his heart, soul, mind and strength in the freedom and fellowship of the Spirit. Far from being frozen in some lifeless pose, the Father, Son and Spirit live in a circle of eager and lavish hospitality. It is a circle of passionate embracing, of mutual acceptance, delight and love, which issues forth not in sadness or depression or misery but in unchained life–joyous, overflowing fellowship. [20]

The patristic Fathers of the early church described The Holy Trinity using a specific term we wish to introduce now... that term is *perichoresis,* [21] which loosely translated means: "rotation." The noun first appears in the writings of St. Maximus Confessor (d. 662). The related verb *perichoreo* is found earlier in the writings of Gregory of Nazianzus (d. 389/90). [22] St. Gregory used it to describe the relationship between the divine and human natures of our Lord Jesus Christ, as did St. John of Damascus (d. 749). John of Damascus extended it to mean the "interpenetration" of the three persons of the Trinity. [23] *Perichoresis* is derived from the Greek *peri,* which means: 'around' and 'chorein' which has multiple meanings – including: 'to make room for', 'go forward' and 'contain'. [24] Author and theologian; Douglas Kelly, comments that if we have ever been to a Greek wedding, we will discover that they have a distinctive way of dancing; a kind of *perichoresis* [25] Kelly explains that in *perichoresis,* there are not two dancers, but at least three. They go in circles, weaving in and out in this very beautiful pattern of motion as they go faster and faster and faster, all the while staying in perfect rhythm and in sync with each other. Eventually, they are dancing so quickly and so effortlessly, that almost becomes a blur. Why is this so important? It is important for its practical impact on human relationships as it is our understanding of the nature of God. It reveals the love of God, the acceptance of God, the being of God.

Genuine acceptance removes fear and hiding and creates freedom to know and be known. In this freedom arises a fellowship and sharing so honest and open and real that persons involved dwell in one another. There is union without loss of individual identity. When one weeps, the other tastes salt. It is only in the Triune relationship of Father, Son and Spirit that personal relationship of this order exists, and the early church used the word *'perichoresis'* to describe it. The good news is that we have been included in this relationship and it is to be played out fully in each of us and in all creation. [26]

LIFE IS DYNAMIC MOVEMENT:
(Consider the Atom)

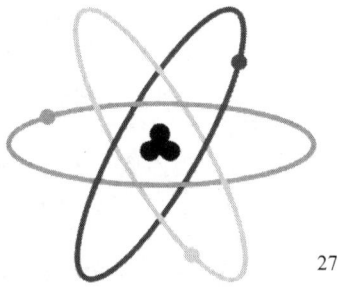

[27]

God is love. God is relationship. God is life. Love, relationship and life all involve dynamic movement. The love and life of God revealed in the perichoretic triune relationship involves dynamic movement. It is not static. Even natural life bears witness to this. God created nature to reflect, in a limited way, His divine attributes.

> ... (wicked men) who by their unrighteousness suppress the truth. For what can be known about God is plain to them, because God has shown it to them. For his invisible attributes, namely, his eternal power and divine nature,

have been clearly perceived, ever since the creation of the world, in the things that have been made. So, they are without excuse (Romans 1:18b-20 ESV).

Nature itself bears witness to God's being and God's invisible attributes – according to the Apostle Paul. Remember, it was Paul who, on Mars Hill, quoted from one of the Greek Philosophers, in His Gospel presentation, in order to convince the Athenians of the reality of the Lord Jesus Christ (Acts 17:28). So, let us quote from 4th century Greek Philosopher, Aristotle, who said that "LIFE IS MOVEMENT," and indeed it is! [28] Movement is fundamental to life. Aristotle had this insight in a pre-scientific world more than two millennia before the discovery of the microscope/before the discovery of atomic theory. [29] Amazing! I'm not a scientist, but I wish to point out that just like THE ATOM (as the basic building block of nature) is essentially "dynamic movement," so likewise is God the Creator of all. Just like an atom is constituted from subatomic particles; protons, neutrons and electrons in dynamic movement and interrelationship, so likewise is the life of the Holy Trinity; Father, Son and Holy Spirit. To make this analogy more accurate, perhaps we should reverse the order. The atom doesn't describe God, rather, God describes the atom. The atom is dynamic movement because that's who (and what) God the Creator is (and not the other way around). God doesn't mimic creation, creation mimics God. The point being that the individual persons of The Holy Trinity are part of a dance; a harmonious relationship of mutual loving, giving, receiving, indwelling and inter-communion. This powerful revelation reveals the essence of God-life/God-love. [30]

> When the Trinity gets pushed to the margin we lose sight of the fact that Christian faith, life and ministry are ultimately participatory [and not simply a matter of correct legal status before God]. We lose sight of the fact

that Christian faith is ultimately union with Christ in the Spirit. When the Trinity slides into the background our understanding of the gospel focuses on forgiveness. However, what Christ did on cross, was not simply to forgive us. It was to restore us to union and communion with the Father, through the Son in the Spirit. All of Christian faith, life and practice is finally participatory. [31] Nietzsche in *Thus Spake Zarathustra* exclaimed that he "could believe only in a God who would know how to dance." The *perichoresis* of God is a dance of love that moves and flows through the ins and outs, ups and downs of all of life's joys and travails. The circle of our dancing is a powerful movement of shared com(passion). Too often in our churches, we want to give dance lessons, to be the judges for dance competitions. But the Lord of the Dance can never be directed or contained. To join the dance of the spirit, we need to break out of our square lines and ballroom boxes and let the spirit draw us in. The dance of the *perichoresis* is a unity of sound and sight, a unity of followers in Jesus, and a unity of God and world. [32]

Christianity, alone among the world faiths, teaches that God is triune. The doctrine of the Trinity is the truth that God is one being existing eternally in three persons: Father, Son and Holy Spirit. The doctrine of the trinity means that God is relational.

INTIMATE FELLOWSHIP
(The closest relationship)

No man hath seen God at any time, *the only begotten Son*, which is *in the bosom of the Father,* he hath declared him. (John 1:18).

Let us consider the intimacy in the triune relationship of God by using other terminology. The Gospel writer John describes the relationship of the Son with the Father in this way. The Son has lived from all eternity in the *"bosom of the Father"* (John 1:18). *"The bosom of the Father"* is an ancient metaphor for love and intimacy. In reference to God, this means that God the Father has loved God the Son (and vice versa) from all eternity. [33] As for another phrase: *"only begotten son,"* this phrase conveys the meaning that God the Son is born of the Father, although uncreated. In other words, the Father is the eternal source of the Son – who is Himself uncreated -and has ever been with the Father. There never was a "time" (to use finite, human forms of expression) when the Father has been without the Son, or the Son without the Father. God has ever been in the holy communion of His tri-personal being from eternity. This is the reason why "God is love." God didn't "become" love, He has always been "love." The trinity reveals this truth.

To say that God is love means that God is relationship! Love requires (a) <u>a giver</u>, (b) <u>a receiver</u>, and (c) <u>the love itself</u>. In the Holy Trinity, the Father is the eternal *lover* and the Son is the eternally *beloved* and the Holy Spirit is the eternal *love of God personally.* We will develop this thought a little later. In John's Gospel, Jesus describes the Holy Spirit as One who "glorifies" him (John 16:14). In turn, the Son glorifies the Father (17:4) and the Father, the Son (17:5). In other words – the Holy Trinity to bring glory to each other. Love is always giving and receiving. It is not selfish. This has been going on for all eternity (17:5b). So then, what does this term "glorify" mean? To glorify someone is to *praise, enjoy and delight in them;* to enjoy them for who they are. Just being in the presence of others is (and ought to be) its own reward. To glorify someone means to serve and prefer them. Instead of sacrificing their interests to make yourself happy, you sacrifice your interests to make them happy. This is the essence of what it means "to glorify" another:

your ultimate joy is to see them joyful and fulfilled. How does this work in the trinity? What does it mean that the Father, Son and Holy Spirit glorify one another? To explain this, we might think of it graphically. Think of being self-centered as being stationary and static. Self-centeredness is when we demand that others orbit around us (i.e. doing things, giving affection to others if it benefits us and our personal goals). God's love is opposite to this. In *perichoresis,* the opposite occurs. *Perichoresis* is the manifestation of true love in which I (the subject) orbit around others (the object) by living in and through them; giving myself for the well-being and benefit of others. This is what defines God-love and God-life.

> Life in the Trinity is characterized by mutual self-giving, not self-centeredness. When we delight, and serve someone else, we enter a dynamic orbit around him or her, we center on the interests and desires of the other. That creates a dance, particularly if there are three persons, each of whom moves around the other two. So, it is, the Bible tells us. Each of the divine person's centers upon the others. None demands that the others revolve around him. Each voluntarily circles the other two, pouring love, delight and adoration into them. [34]

[35]

LIFE IN THE TRINITY:
(The forgotten heart of the faith)

Why have we been saved and forgiven of our sins? Answer: to be welcomed and included into the family of God. It is from a sense of Divine belonging and secure love that true inner transformation occurs. We cannot guilt-monger someone into meaningful, lasting change! We cannot fear-monger someone into meaningful, lasting change. Paul said: *"... it is God's kindness that is leading you to repent."* (Romans 2:4 ISV). John said: *"Dear friends, now we are children of God, and what we will be has not yet been made known. But we know that when Christ appears, we shall be like him, for we shall see him as he is" (1 John 3:2 NIV).* Here is the goal of forgiveness. Forgiveness is ultimately about a pathway to reconciliation and inclusion – to bring us back into right relationship in the family of God. While forgiveness may be instant, reconciliation takes time. The goal of forgiveness is reconciliation eventually. Forgiveness and reconciliation are related, but they are two different things.

Forgiveness always precedes reconciliation, but forgiveness does not necessarily guarantee reconciliation. The motivation of forgiveness is the hope of reconciliation. Forgiveness is one-sided. Reconciliation is two-sided. God has forgiven us (already) in Christ for reconciliation – as we receive the gift of the Holy Spirit and trust in the work of the cross. By grace, we become sons and daughters of God and become partakers of the love and life of God through grace, which is ours through the indwelling Holy Spirit (Romans 5:5) who secures our adoption in Christ (Romans 8:15). The reason Jesus came to earth is that we might share in the life and love of God through Him. This is the reason for the incarnation. To accomplish this, God in Christ had to save us first; save us from sin and death. But salvation <u>FROM</u> sin and death is only half the story. Salvation <u>TO</u> life and fellowship is the rest of the story. The full-scope of this glorious truth is often overlooked as many evangelicals only focus on the first half of this equation. We have been forgiven to become partakers of the life of God in Christ. This is the heart of the Gospel. Christianity is much more than forgiveness and behavior modification. Christianity is not just a moral code (although it is the ultimate morality). Christianity is not just a philosophy (although it is the ultimate "love of wisdom" *[philosophy means: "love of wisdom")*. Christianity is not only a religion (although it is the "pure and undefiled religion," per James 1:27. What is Christianity? Answer: Christianity is above all the life of God in Christ whereby redeemed mankind has been made partakers of the life of God: *"made partakers of the Divine nature" (2 Peter 1:4)* through the gift of the Holy Spirit. The reason for the incarnation was to redeem mankind to bring us into the loving embrace of the Father. This is the essence of the parable of the Prodigal Son. Being restored to the Father's embrace is what life is all about! In such an experience, we begin to *"know the love that surpasses knowledge" (Ephesians 3:19),* as Paul states it. God finds delight in His children! God delights in you! Why is this so? Not because our behavior always pleases Him – it does not! Rather, God finds delight in us because we are made *imago Dei* ("in the image of God"). Consider this:

> God created man in His own image, in the image of God He created him; male and female He created them. (Genesis 1:27 NASB).

Jesus the man (in His humanity), knew who He was in relation to His Heavenly Father. We too must come to know who we are in relation to the Father. The truest thing about us is who we are in Christ! God has already embraced us in Christ. Because JESUS IS "FACE TO FACE" with the Father, so are we "in Him." He is our representative. Christ is the titular head of the New Creation. We are new creatures in Christ. This is the great Pauline revelation presented in the New Testament.

> You will not find your identity in what you have, but in who has you. You will not find your identity in what you do, but in what has been done for you. And you will not find your identity in what you desire, but in who has desired—at infinite cost to Himself—a relationship with you. Christ is your life. He gives you a new identity and will work that new identity out in your life until the day when He appears. On that day, you will finally see clearly, as Christ sees you now. You will know as you are known. And you will understand that the truest thing about you—that in Christ God called you His beloved in whom He is well pleased—has been true all along. And is now true forever. Believe. Trust. Base your entire identity on that fact. ~ *David Lomas* [36]

FACE TO FACE WITH GOD:
(Jesus our representative)

In the words of the well-known hymn: *"Face to face with Christ my Savior, face to face what will it be,"* [37] let us consider the holy meaning of this awesome concept. Before we may consider what, it means to go face to face with God – we should understand what it means for Jesus Himself, as the only begotten Son; the eternal Logos. The eternal Son has ever been "face to face" with the Father. This is why Jesus is uniquely our representative. Only the Son can bring us face-to-face with the Father, because only the Son <u>knows</u> the Father, and only the Son <u>reveals</u> the Father!

"In the beginning was the Word, and the Word was <u>with</u> God, and the Word was God" (John 1:1 KJV). *(Greek translation below):* [38]

John's use of "with" (Gr. πρὸς pros) in Jn.1:1-2 is unique. If John had used the dative case, it would mean something like the Word was "with God" or even "at God's place" (in the sense of the French *chez moi*), for that is the typical usage. The use of πρὸς in John 1:1-2 is a very unusual one, and it defies English translation, although "face to face" is close, even though the idea of "a face" (as such) is not in the preposition. "Directed, oriented towards (on a common level)" is closer to the idea, although this too is hard to work into an English translation. St. John, under the guidance of the Holy Spirit, has gone to great lengths (i.e. coming up with this inspired use of πρὸς) to make clear that while the Word was in the presence of God, the Word was also separate from God the Father, but at the same time not inferior to God the Father. [39]

The amazing truth about the incarnation and Calvary is that we have a "face to face" relationship with God in Christ by grace – because Jesus the incarnate Son has this relationship with the Father by nature. To be clear here: we have no independent relationship with God. Rather, we have a dependent and contingent relationship with God in Christ. We are not "gods" in an independent sort of way (which was the Serpent's lie in Genesis 3:5 *"you will become as gods…"* Rather, we become "sons of God" by grace in Christ. Jesus became who we are so that we might become who He is. Again, that is <u>not</u> to say that we somehow assume independent deity, but rather, we become "sons of God" by grace through faith because of our adoption "in Christ".

For now, we see in a mirror dimly, <u>but then face to face</u>. Now I know in part; then I shall know fully, even as I have been fully known (1 Corinthians 13:12).

And <u>they shall see his face</u>; and his name shall be in their foreheads (Revelation 22:4).
Beloved, we are God's children now, and what we will be has not yet appeared; but we know that when he appears, we shall be like him, because we shall see him as he is (1 John 3:2).

Herein is our love made perfect, that we may have boldness in the day of judgment: because as he is, so are we in this world (1 John 4:17).

HIS IDENTITY AND OURS:
(So are we in this world)

The Beloved Apostle John said: *"... as he is, so also are we in this world." (1 John 4:17 ESV).* To know Christ's identity is essential for us to understand our identity in Christ. Jesus (the Logos) is God's only begotten Son by nature. Jesus is the ONLY begotten Son in eternity (from un-beginning). In Jesus Christ, we are made sons of God by grace; adopted in time because of the work of Calvary through the infilling of the Holy Spirit. Let us consider now Jesus' identity as the eternal Son; the Logos, in His relation to the Father. This is important because of such heretical/apostate groups as the Jehovah's Witness, Mormons and others – which deny the eternal deity of Jesus Christ. For the Jehovah's Witness sect, their New World Translation of the Bible inaccurately translates John 1:1 from the Greek. [40] Therefore, a proper exegesis is necessary: *"My people perish for lack of knowledge"* (Hosea 4:6).

- **ERROR:** (New World Translation): *"and the Word was with God, and the Word was <u>a god</u>."* [41]
- **TRUTH:** (King James Version): *"and the Word was with God, and the Word <u>was God</u>."*
- **TRUTH:** (Greek literal rendering): "and the Word was *[ēn]* with *[pros]* the God *[ton theon]*, and God *[theos]* was the Word."

The above detail matters because it vitally affects our relationship with God. This is not mere abstract theology. The truth is this: only "God" Himself can bring us face to face with "God." Only God (the incarnate Son) can bring us face to face with God (the Father). In this way, Jesus Christ is our only representative, intercessor and mediator ("the man Christ Jesus" – 1 Timothy 2:5) who is *"God from God, Light from Light, true God from true God, begotten, not made, one in Being with the Father,"* [42] can bring us face to face with the God the Father. If Jesus was something less than God by nature, then we (the redeemed) could not become sons of God by grace. St. Athanasius (4th century) said: *"He (Christ) became what we are that we might become what he is."* This describes, better than most statements, the motivation for creation and redemption in Christ. Fallen humanity needed more than forgiveness and pardon. Fallen humanity needed new creation – which God in Christ initiated through the incarnation.

NEW CREATION IN CHRIST:
(The One for the many)

Forgiveness is only half the equation. "Repentance cannot remedy fallen nature: we are corrupted and need to be restored to the grace of God's image, and no one can renew but he who created. He alone could recreate all, suffer for all, represent all before the Father. The Word visits the earth, where he has always been present, and sees its evil condition. He takes a human body, born of a pure virgin in whose womb he makes human flesh his own, in which to reveal himself, conquer death, and restore life." [43] This is the reason for Christ's death and resurrection. In the resurrection, Jesus becomes THE GOOD NEWS. In the resurrection, the Church announces the good news of salvation and hope for mankind throughout the ages. Christ's resurrection is the first and decisive moment in the life of the church which lives and moves toward it through the power of the Spirit until that final day [44] at Christ's Second Coming when corruption shall put on incorruption and mortality shall put on immortality. Christ's resurrection prefigures and guarantees our resurrection. Consider here the words of C.S. Lewis and others on this important theme:

> To become new men means losing what we now call 'ourselves.' Out of ourselves, into Christ, we must go... the Christian life is simply a process of having your natural self-changed into a Christ self... One's most private wishes, one's point of view, are the things that have to be changed." (C.S. Lewis in "Mere Christianity"). Our natural self-changed into a Christ-self. We invite Jesus Christ to enter our lives and to be formed in us, and thus, become mirrors of Christ. We become little "Christs" in the world around us. We fulfill the potential that He has placed in each one of us when He created us in His likeness. Of course, such change implies something radical happening in us; it demands us to crucify our own ego, our egocentric ways and live according to Christ. And such change continues throughout our life, it becomes life-long transformation. New life in Christ may seem to have a sudden beginning, but it is a progressive reality of daily transformation as we come into the likeness of Christ (2 Corinthians 3:18). [45] That is why Paul reminds us of Adam: to give us a clue,

a mental handhold from which we can begin to grope toward imagining how our destiny can be determined by action of a single great figure who comes before us and shapes the reality in which we live. But the Adam-Christ analogy should never mislead us into thinking that Jesus Christ merely undoes the effects of Adam's transgressions and puts us back to square one with a blank slate. Instead, Jesus has swept us into a new creation so that our identity is now positively redefined by His faithfulness and not our own disloyalty to God. [46]

A great truth about the incarnation can be seen in the prodigal son parable. In His incarnation, Jesus came "face to face" with us, in our fallen-ness. Jesus relived Adam's life backwards and in so doing rebooted the human-race.

> *A world of nice people, content in their own niceness, looking no further, turned away from God, would be just as desperately in need of salvation as a miserable world— and might even be more difficult to save. God became man to turn creatures into sons: not simply to produce better men of the old kind but to produce a new kind of man.* – C.S. Lewis, Mere Christianity [47]

> [Christ] was in these last days, according to the time appointed by the Father, united to His own workmanship, inasmuch as He became a man liable to suffering ... He commenced afresh1 the long line of human beings, and furnished us, in a brief, comprehensive manner, with salvation; so, that what we had lost in Adam—namely, to be according to the image and likeness of God—that we might recover in Christ Jesus. – Irenaeus of Lyons [48]

Jesus accomplished what He accomplished to take us "face to face" with God. When Jesus embraced humanity (in the incarnation), He made a way for redeemed humanity to embrace the Father in Him. This is how we are made new creations in Christ. This is what it means to be the "new mankind." All things have become new in Christ. Christ's incarnation, life, death, resurrection, ascension and session at the Father's right hand has literally changed the course of human history. Paul said in Romans 6 and elsewhere: we have been crucified, buried, risen, ascended and seated with Him in heavenly places in Christ! It is an objective fact in Christ.

> Therefore, we were buried with Him through baptism into death, that just as Christ was raised from the dead by the glory of the Father, even so we also should walk in newness of life. For if we have been united together in the likeness of His death, certainly we also shall be in the likeness of His resurrection (Romans 6:4-5). But God, who is rich in mercy, because of His great love with which He loved us, even when we were dead in trespasses, made us alive together with Christ (by grace you have been saved), and raised us up together, and made us sit together in the heavenly places in Christ Jesus (Ephesians 2:4-6).

GOD'S ESSENTIAL NATURE:
(Unconditional love)

The story of the parable of the prodigal son reveals the glorious truth of who we are in Christ. As with all the parables, they convey a heavenly meaning using an early story. A parable is essentially an earthly story with a heavenly meaning. The parable of the Prodigal Son is a story about the redeeming and reconciling love of God. If we look at the overriding theme of

Scripture, both old and new, we arrive at this conclusion: The essence of who God is both in eternity and redemptive history is summed up in this: GOD IS LOVE! Because God is love, therefore, God saves! God's great salvation is a result of His great love. God has saved us in Christ in history, and He is continually sanctifying us through the work of the indwelling Spirit. We have been saved to share in the Divine fellowship of the Father and Son through the Spirit. Peter puts it this way...

> Through these he has given us his very great and precious promises, so that through them you may participate in the divine nature, having escaped the corruption in the world caused by evil desires (2 Peter 1:4 NIV).

The apostle John articulated God's essential nature in 1 John 4:8 and 16 ("God is love"). Love is the meaning of life. Commenting on this, St. Teresa of Avila said: *"It is love alone that gives worth to all things."* [49] The love of God is the meaning and logic of creation. Because God is love – everything else has worth and value. For this reason, even fallen humanity is worthy of rescue, redemption and recreation in the sight of God. Therefore, the incarnation had to take place. That is why the Son of God "emptied Himself" (*the kenosis*) for our salvation. The *kenosis* demonstrates what love <u>does</u> – how love acts! Love seeks the highest good of another. It is the self-sacrificial action of the lover toward the beloved. Love "gives." Love is self-giving, self-emptying and always other-centered and other-empowering. Paul explains it this way in Philippians.

> Let nothing be done through selfish ambition or conceit, but in lowliness of mind let each esteem others better than himself. Let each of you look out not only for his own interests, but also for the interests of others. Let this mind be in you which was also in Christ Jesus, who, being

in the form of God, did not consider it robbery to be equal with God, but made Himself of no reputation, taking the form of a bondservant, and coming in the likeness of men. And being found in appearance as a man, He humbled Himself and became obedient to the point of death, even the death of the cross. Therefore, God also has highly exalted Him and given Him the name which is above every name, that at the name of Jesus every knee should bow, of those in heaven, and of those on earth, and of those under the earth, and that every tongue should confess that Jesus Christ is Lord, to the glory of God the Father. [50]

THROUGH THE LOOKING GLASS:
(The Jesus model)

In the famous book by Lewis Carroll, *Through the Looking Glass,* Alice steps through the living room mirror to find a world on the opposite side where everything is backwards. In the story, Alice wants to go forward, but every time she moves, she ends up back where she started. She tries to go left and ends up right. In that world, up is down and fast is slow. This is how it is in the Kingdom of God. Christianity is a kind of *looking glass world* where everything works on principles that are contrary to those of the fallen, sin-depraved world around us. Everything is in reverse. Life in our fallen world is upside-down. Jesus came to turn the upside-down world, right-side up.

> And when they could not find them, they dragged Jason and some of the brothers before the city authorities, shouting, "These men who have turned the world upside down have come here also" (Acts 17:6 ESV).

Jesus came into the world to reveal what has been described as the "upside down" kingdom. Jesus is the King who won by serving. He triumphed by losing. It's backward to the world. To be blessed, we bless others. To receive love, we give love. To be honored, we first become humble. To truly live, we die to self. To gain the unseen, we let go of the seen. To receive, we first give. To save our life, we lose it. To lead, we become a servant. To be first, we become last... and so on... [51] [52] The message of grace pervades the entire New Testament. The concept of unmerited favor is in direct opposition to performance. This favor isn't due to a lack of effort but to a lack of earning. Grace is one of the most basic teachings of Jesus, yet so many of us have difficulty in fully embracing unearned favor. We also dangerously bring this understanding of success into our kingdom pursuits. When we use numbers and metrics in direct relation to our definition of success, we can miss what God is doing behind the numbers. [53]

THE 7-FOLD EMPTYING
(the seven-downs):

1. Did not consider it robbery to be equal with God (ESV translation: who, though he was in the form of God, did not count equality with God a thing to be grasped") (NIV translation: "did not consider equality with God something to be used to his own advantage")
2. Made Himself of no reputation
3. Taking the form of a bondservant
4. Coming in the likeness of man
5. He humbled Himself
6. Became obedient to the point of death
7. Even the death of the cross

THE 7-FOLD EXALTATION
(the seven-ups):

1. God has highly exalted Him
2. Given Him a name which is above every name
3. That at the name of Jesus, every knee should bow
4. Of those in heaven
5. Of those in earth
6. Of those under the earth
7. Every tongue should confess that Jesus Christ is Lord to the glory of God the Father

LOVE, GLORY AND ELECTION:
(Jesus is Lord of all)

In the above Philippians text, notice the last point concerning Christ's exaltation. The climax of God's self-giving nature is the universal proclamation that Jesus Christ is Lord of all. The Lordship of Jesus Christ becomes the universal confession and submission of every creature in heaven, on earth and under the earth, in other words: everywhere in creation. Here is where we find the Father's glory revealed. The self-giving love of the Father towards Jesus the Son in the Holy Spirit is the ultimate manifestation of God's glory. Here is an important theological point that many have overlooked. The glory of God must never be set 'over-against' the love of God! Quite the opposite. The glory of God IS His self-giving love. Philippians 2:1-11 makes this abundantly clear. Much otherwise fine preaching today fails to combine these two critical elements. When we preach about God's *glory, providence and election,* we must INCLUDE the truth that God's glory IS His *goodness and love.* And now for a further step in this understanding – because God is love, God has elected all mankind in Jesus Christ; the One for the many. Simply put, election in its basic definition means: "choice." God has chosen us "in Christ," not some of us, but all of us. Every human being, the entire race of Adam, has been chosen in Christ. This is an important revelation which we will now attempt to brief explain.

> Church Father, Gregory of Palamas, said: "God does not decide what men's will shall be. It is not that He foreordains and thus foreknows, but that He foreknows and thus foreordains, and not by His will but by His knowledge of what we shall freely will or choose." [54]

For clarity, let us say to our students that the theology we are teaching is grounded in the patristics; what is sometimes called Trinitarian [55] or Incarnational-Trinitarian theology. It is theology that is pre-reformation in origin and thus neither strictly Calvinist or Arminian because it pre-dates that period in church history and the arguments that gave rise to those specific western church classifications. Trinitarian theology finds truth in both sides of that 16th century debate, but limits itself to neither. Some have described Trinitarian theology as the third option (what we call: the original option). The protestant world has been programmed to think primarily in terms of Calvinism versus Arminianism, as if nothing else existed before these 16th century debates and terms.

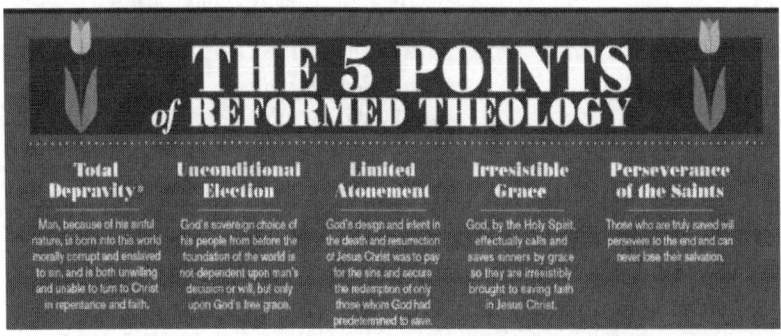

[56] [57]

KNOWING THE FATHER'S HEART

In the 20th century, such luminary figures as Karl Barth and T.F. Torrance; Reformed theologians, became leading proponents of modified Calvinism; what is sometimes referred to as "Evangelical Calvinism." What Barth, in part, and Torrance, especially, did was look back for inspiration to the earlier theology of the Eastern Church, which represents the earliest tradition of the Christian church.

[58]

John Calvin /   Jacob Arminius   / Thomas F. Torrance

This subject is too big for thorough reflection here and now. For more comprehensive meditation upon Trinitarian theology, [59] we encourage students to visit the helpful website of Grace Communion International (www.gci.org) as a good starting point. Let us highlight a few things here and now which should aid our understanding of God's Father Heart as depicted in the prodigal son parable. According to Trinitarian theology, Jesus is the Elect One, and all humanity is elect in Him. In other words, our election is "in Christ," not separate from Him. This is not only the proper way to understand election, but the proper way to understand God's unconditional love. God does NOT elect some to salvation and others to damnation. That's not how election works, neither is that the action of Divine love.

> The doctrine of election involves two aspects, the electing God and the elected man. As the electing God, the Father, the Son, and the Holy Spirit together make a choice. The choice God makes is that the Son of God will

become the elected man, Jesus of Nazareth. The Triune God eternally elects, or chooses, in divine freedom, to be for humanity the God of grace and love. Therefore, in Jesus Christ, who is fully God and fully man, God is both the elector and the elected. Karl Barth explained it this way: "Jesus Christ is both the electing God and elected man in One." Theologian and Barth scholar John Webster, describes it as: "God elects to be this God, God in this man, God known in and as Jesus Christ." As the act of grace and love, the Son of God is elected to give of himself to become united with the Son of Man for the specific purpose to save sinful humans. This is the act of free grace where God gives "love in the deepest condescension," that is, he reaches down to pull humans to himself. The Son of God empties and humbles himself so that humans may be united in fellowship with God (Philippians 2:6-8; John 17:22-24). [60]

For Barth, the doctrine of election is the sum of the gospel, for it reveals the heart of God: "God's eternal will is the election of Jesus Christ". He is the loving God who has freely chosen and created human beings to be in his image and in fellowship with him. This is the absolute good news. There is no bad news mixed with the good news, no fear mixed with terror, no certainty mixed with uncertainty. We are not left to blind fate or some unknown will of God. Our election and predestination by God is certain in Jesus Christ, and in him alone and in him fully we have and know the will of God for the meaning and direction of our lives. [61]

"God is not a capricious tyrant who elects some to salvation and elect's others to perdition by some abstract absolute decree. Such a *supralapsarian* God threatens to take on the appearance of a demon – which quite naturally makes many Christians recoil; including Catholics, Orthodox and a great many Protestants," [62] and so it should! We dare not distort the loving face of God into a cosmic ogre; a moral monster. There can be no division of humanity into two groups—the "elect" and the "rejected," according to Barth. God has saved us all in Christ. This is the Good News of the Gospel! And yet, some portion of humanity will nevertheless be lost (as irrational and as inexplicable as this may be) because of personal choice. The Scripture is clear about this. *"Whosoever will, let him come" (Revelation 22:17).* The gates of the city will never be shut (Revelation 21:25). This is an important revelation about the attitude of God in the finished work of Calvary. Heaven is open, but God will allow unbelievers to deny the truth (i.e. deny their acceptance/election in Christ) and continue living "the lie" forever in hell, which is a state of their own making. Karl Barth put this way: "Hell is the unbeliever's unreality into eternity, even though he/she is accepted by God and elected by God in Jesus Christ. God will not force him or her to be in heaven with him." [63]

C. S. Lewis, in his excellent book entitled: "The Great Divorce," explained hell as "the painful refuge" whose door is locked on the inside because man's choices are real. That being true, however, we should never confuse man's choices as capable of nullifying God's will. Man's choices in salvation are NOT about the efficacy or extent of Calvary's work – only about whether we individually believe and receive it. To reject our salvation in Christ is to live in unreality. It is important to state at this point that the author does not espouse "universalism" *(universal reconciliation – a.k.a. apokatastasis);* [64] which is a heresy that was condemned by the early church back in the sixth century CE. That being said, Christ's work on the cross is a finished work, and it accomplished precisely what it purposed for all those it was intended. In the cross, mankind (all mankind) was objectively included in Christ. However, we must now individually, subjectively, acknowledge our salvation in Christ and thus experience the "new creation" which is already ours in Christ. To do otherwise is to continue to live in "the lie." For Barth, this is an epistemological issue and not an ontological one; everyone is included in the free grace of God in Jesus Christ – however, God will allow those who insist on rejecting their acceptance by Him to go to hell if they so choose. In the words of C.S. Lewis, in the end – there are only two categories of people: (a) those who say to God, *"thy will be done"* – and enter heaven, and (b) those to whom God says, *"thy will be done"* – and enter hell. [65] The complete quote is in the footnotes. This brings us back to the topic of God's unconditional love and reminds us of an important statement made by the Old Testament prophet Jonah. We might remember the primary complaint of Jonah; the rebellious prophet, in regards to God's character in God's dealing with wicked Nineveh. Jonah made this statement:

> That is why I made haste to flee to Tarshish; for I knew that you are a gracious God and merciful, slow to anger and abounding in steadfast love, and relenting from disaster. (John 4:2).

Jonah learned of this essential truth about God's essential nature and character (i.e. that He is "gracious, merciful and abounding in steadfast love") from the law at Sinai. We don't often think of this fact (many people assume the law does not reveal the love of God). Jonah (and all Old Testament prophets) were essentially interpreters/proclaimers of God's covenant and law (given on Mt. Sinai). It was there that God revealed His essential nature to Moses, at his request: "show me Your glory". To that excellent question – God answered Moses: *"I will cause all my goodness to pass before you..."* (Exodus 33:19). The answer that God gave to Moses' question was another way of saying: "God is love." The love of God is everywhere in the

Bible; used hundreds of times throughout the Old Testament through the phrase (or some version of it): "His mercy endures forever; His everlasting love endures forever." In fact, forty-seven times, the psalms speak of God's "steadfast love." In comparison to God's *love,* God's *justice* comes in a distant second in the number of occurrences we find in Scripture. This primary emphasis is quite interesting. God's *justice* and His *love* should be seen in parallel terms, not antithetical to one another. God is love because He is just and God is just because He is love. Consider Exodus 33.

> 14 The Lord replied, "My Presence will go with you, and I will give you rest." 15 Then Moses said to him, "If your Presence does not go with us, do not send us up from here. 16 How will anyone know that you are pleased with me and with your people unless you go with us? What else will distinguish me and your people from all the other people on the face of the earth?" 17 And the Lord said to Moses, "I will do the very thing you have asked, because I am pleased with you and I know you by name." 18 Then Moses said, "Now show me your glory." 19 And the Lord said, "I will cause all my goodness to pass in front of you, and I will proclaim my name, the Lord, in your presence. I will have mercy on whom I will have mercy, and I will have compassion on whom I will have compassion. [66]

Professor Victor Furnish (Southern Methodist University) said that "God's love is <u>not</u> like a heat-seeking missile attracted to something inherently attractive in this or that person." God's other-directed love bestows worth, honor, even glory. Psalm 8.5 says, *"God has made us but a little less than God"* (or another reading would be, *"than the angels" "and crowned human beings with glory and honor."*) Apparently, man's exaltation does not subtract from God's glory, but adds to it. God, it would appear, is not merely a glory-grabber, but rather a glory-giver." [67] Again, the glory of God and the election of God are not at odds with the love of God. This is important for Protestants to remember, especially when we consider the foundational statements of the Reformation; particularly: *The Five Solas* – and specifically the 5th: *Soli Deo Gloria* (glory to God alone).

THE PRIMARY DOCTRINE:
(Trinitarian Love)

God's love <u>is</u> His glory! This concept is often at odds with classic five-point Calvinism; which usually includes the doctrine of double predestination. [68] For them, it is difficult to speak of God's love, on the one hand, and speak of God's predestination of some portion of humanity to eternal damnation, on the other hand. How to reconcile the love of God with the *destinare ad peccatum* (i.e. that God predestinates some to sin and eternal damnation) is the great conundrum for classic (federal) Calvinists. John Calvin himself taught this (see the endnotes), [69] although in other places he seems to soften his stance. We have several problems with classic (federal) Calvinism; including but not limited to: (1) It relies on a faulty application of Scripture, in some instances, [70] (2) It sometimes deviates from the Ecumenical Councils and the Church Fathers, (3) It teaches God's sovereignty in such a way as to lead to a *defacto* denial of God's unconditional love for all men, (4) It has a western-church view of the Trinity. [71] To elaborate on these points is far beyond the scope of our current study. But we simply mention them as a point of historical reference. We should understand that the Reformation was basically a reaction against the excesses of Roman Catholicism; and particularly papal indulgences. Most dogmas of the Christian church throughout history are set over/against heretical extremes to which they were reacting. The same is true with the Protestant Reformation – which was a

Catholic Reformation (all the magisterial reformers were in fact, Catholic). The term Protestant didn't come into being until later. The point we wish to make is that the Reformers (in our opinion) did not pay close enough attention to the other half of Christianity (i.e. the original side of Christianity; Eastern Orthodoxy) in their diligent search for a corrective to the corrupted Roman Catholicism of their day. They were reacting against Romanism and as such, put their focus on soteriological issues (matters of salvation) and emphasized the doctrine of "justification by faith" as the *primaria doctrinae* (primary doctrine) in reaction to the error of papal indulgences. It is our contention that the Reformers did not pay close enough attention to the doctrine of God in the tradition of the Eastern Fathers, which emphases the Trinity.

If the reformers had paid closer attention to the Eastern Fathers, they would have emphasized the priority of the Trinity which preeminently reveals the love of God. In our opinion, this is still a major problem within our contemporary western churches. We have the same lingering problem. Our soteriology must first run through the filter of our theology. A proper theology precedes a proper soteriology. How we understand God Himself, influences how we understand God's great salvation in Christ. Who God IS (His essence) precedes what God HAS DONE (His action). To the patristic church, the doctrine of the Trinity took priority – including a robust Christology. It is interesting to note that atonement theories (i.e. soteriology) never became a matter of ecumenical dogma in the seven ecumenical councils. [72] A review of the first four ecumenical councils of the One, Holy, Apostolic and Catholic church reveals the veracity of these statements. The ecumenical councils were primarily about the nature and character of God (Who He is). The ecumenical councils were primarily Theocentric, and specifically Christocentric. Again, we say, before we can properly understand the *work* of Christ (soteriology – which includes the doctrine of "justification by faith"), we must FIRST understand the *nature* of God (theology) and Christ (Christology). The contemporary protestant church has in some instances, forgotten this priority. Now let us briefly show why. The Patristic Fathers, over the course of the first eight-centuries of the Christian era, gave primary attention to a proper Christology (who is Christ), which required a proper theology (who is God in Trinity). This should give the contemporary church great pause to once again reconsider the priority of Christo-centric, Trinitarian doctrine.

73

- The First Council of Nicaea (A.D. 325) was essentially about the doctrine of God (the Trinity) – focus on the divinity of God the Son.
- The First Council of Constantinople (A.D. 381) was essentially about the doctrine of God (the Trinity) – focus on the divinity of God the Holy Spirit.

- The Council of Ephesus (A.D. 431) was essentially about the doctrine of God (the Trinity) – focus on the truth of the one divine person in Christ.
- The Council of Chalcedon (A.D. 451) was about the doctrine of God (the Trinity) – focus on the truth that there are two natures (human and divine) in the one divine person of God the Son.

The fifth ecumenical council basically reiterated the dogmas of the third and fourth councils. The sixth ecumenical council gave further definition to the "two wills" in Christ. The seventh ecumenical council dealt with the issue of iconoclasm in seeking properly define the image (icon) of God. So, there we have it. The nature and character of God was at the center of patristic discussion for the first eight centuries of the Christian era. Modern author and Protestant scholar; Dr. Donald Fairbairn, brings balance to the contemporary Protestant church in his excellent book entitled: "Life in the Trinity," [74] in which he points out that the central truth of the Gospel is WHO IS GOD (as Trinity); a blessed truth best expressed, not by the Reformers, but by the Patristic Fathers.

> Part of the reason we tend to regard theology, doctrine, as being somewhat irrelevant to Christian life is that our theological discussions tend to focus on the doctrines themselves rather than on the God to whom those doctrines point. Thus, students and others substitute truths about God for God. Many protestants today see the study of God as an academic exercise rather than to make the experience of God the goal of life. This tendency harkens back to the Scholasticism that marked the Middle Ages. [75]

We need to study God to know God as He is and not just "about" Him. We must know God as He, is to experience His personal presence in purity, holiness and love. Fairbairn explains that whereas much modern theology argues that we should trust the Bible because we can prove its reliability, the Patristic Fathers "assumed" the authority of Scripture, not because they could prove it to be reliable, but because it came from God Himself. For the Fathers, it was much more than an intellectual exercise, it was a personal matter of faith. Fairbairn sees this as a greater act of submission to God than most modern theology. [76] The contemporary church must get back to the focus on the God of the Scriptures, and not merely the Scriptures about God. God is intensely personal and not just an academic pursuit. God is not Father, Son and Holy Bible (I say this tongue in cheek, of course), but rather Father, Son and Holy Spirit. The early church avoided the problem of divorcing *doctrine* from *Christian life* by understanding that all Christian living is primarily a direct connection to God's own life. The focus of the fathers was not on doctrine itself, but on God in whose life we share, [77] and Who correct doctrine reveals.

MONARCHY OF THE FATHER:
(Practical Implications)

A further challenge we find in western theology is the notion of thinking of God in a *non-personal* way (i.e. as a unified substance or essence) in the first instance. We tend to follow the classical, scientific, Aristotelian approach in western theology which places God's essence, or substance *(ousia)* as primary, whereas in eastern theology, the person *(hypostasis)* of the Father is primary. At first, this may seem inconsequential, but it is not. Western Church theology begins with God's impersonal *ousia* and then works backwards into His triune *hypostasis*, whereas the Eastern Church does theology beginning with the Father's Monarchy (i.e. the person of the Father as the starting point) and then works into the triune relationship; the

Son only begotten, and the Spirit ever-proceeding. Orthodox theologian John Ziziouslas explains it this way:

> In our thinking about the divine Trinity, we must (like the Cappadocian fathers) start with the concept of the person. It is the three persons who together constitute the one being of God. The notion of the one divine substance is not ontologically prior to the concept of the person. It is rather the other way around because the divine substance exists only as persons. The real being of God is not somewhere behind or beyond the Father, the Son and the Holy Spirit, but precisely in the mutual communion of these three persons. [78]

The Western Church (both Catholic and Protestant), by starting with the one substance/essence of God (in prioritizing God's unity over His persons), tends to arrive at a non-personal, non-relational, and thus non-loving conclusion. This is not intentional – but this is the result. Therefore, western theology tends towards a legal, forensic understanding of God, which emphases justice over love. The point is this – our theological starting point influences our theological ending point. The Eastern Church, by focusing primarily on the monarchy of the Father (as the *arche* and source of the Son and Spirit) arrives at a relational understanding of God. This in turn reveals the love of God clearly and unambiguously. This personal understanding shines the light on God's gracious character which is the point of Jesus' Prodigal Son parable. Focusing on the triune persons of the Godhead reveals the love of God, and explains WHY God is love. God is love because God is a tri-personal being; (i.e.) able to give and receive love from the other persons within the godhead in whom the Father has eternal relationship. This may be the most important theological truth.

The fact that the Father, Son, and Holy Spirit are distinct Persons means, in other words, that the Father is not the Son, the Son is not the Holy Spirit, and the Holy Spirit is not the Father. Jesus is God, but He is not the Father or the Holy Spirit. The Holy Spirit is God, but He is not the Son or the Father. They are different Persons, not three different ways of looking at God. The personhood of each member of the Trinity means that each Person has a distinct center of consciousness. Thus, they relate to each other personally — the Father regards Himself as "I" while He regards the Son and Holy Spirit as "You." Likewise, the Son regards Himself as "I," but the Father and the Holy Spirit as "You." Often it is objected that "if Jesus is God, then he must have prayed to himself while he was on earth." But the answer to this objection lies in simply applying what we have already seen. While Jesus and the Father are both God, they are different Persons. Thus, Jesus prayed to God the Father without praying to Himself. In fact, it is precisely the continuing dialog between the Father and the Son (Matthew 3:17; 17:5; John 5:19; 11:41–42; 17:1ff) which furnishes the best evidence that they are distinct Persons with distinct centers of consciousness. [79]

IDENTITY AND DESTINY:
(Life in the Spirit)

Mankind is made *imago Dei* (meaning: "in the image of God"). The image of God in mankind is the primary difference between mankind and the rest of creation. The image of God is also what distinguishes mankind from our Creator. The *imago Dei* both distinguishes us and links us to our Creator. It does both. While the Bible says that mankind is created in the image of God, mankind is NOT (just to be clear) the very image of God. The very image of God is something reserved exclusively for

Jesus Christ. In contrast – we are image bearers. Jesus is the very image of God (Colossians 1:5; Hebrews 1:1-3) in whose image we are a mere reflection. *"No one has ever seen God, but the one and only Son, who is Himself God and is in closest relationship with the Father, has made him known" (John 1:18 NIV).* The Greek word for the English phrase: "made him known" is *exēgēsato,* which means: *"to explain, to declare, to unfold, to narrate, to show the way."* [80] Jesus is the only one who declares, explains and shows us the Father. *"All things have been handed over to me by my Father, and no one knows the Son except the Father, and no one knows the Father except the Son and anyone to whom the Son chooses to reveal him" (Matthew 11:27 ESV).* There is a direct link between mankind and Jesus Christ. If all humanity is created *imago Dei* and initially exercised dominion over the earth (Genesis 1:28, a role within creation like God the Son, who exercises dominion over creation – and all humanity and God the Son are linked by virtue of the *imago Dei),* then all human beings are meant to share in the Son's relationship with the Father. In Genesis 2 we are given more detail about the creation of Adam.

After God formed Adam from the dust of the earth, He breathed into Adam the breath of life (literally "lives" – plural) and man became a "living soul." This is like Jesus' words after His resurrection in John 20:21-22. After commissioning His disciples, the Bible says that Jesus breathed on His disciples saying: "Receive the Holy Spirit." Fairbairn sees similarities here between Genesis 2:7 and John 20:21-22 and concludes that God did not only breath the "breath of life" (i.e. "mortal life") into Adam, but the Spirit of life Himself (i.e. the Holy Spirit) into Adam. God gave Adam the Holy Spirit and thereby linked Adam to Jesus; in whose image Adam was created, thereby causing him to share in the fellowship of the Holy Trinity. In the same way, today, when God gives His redeemed children the gift of the Holy Spirit, and thus restores us to a state like the original state in which we share in the life of the Holy Trinity; a life that Adam and Eve lost in The Fall. This is essentially the meaning of death. Death is essentially "separation from the life of God," which is why the New Testament sometimes speaks of Believers merely *falling asleep.* Death has lost its sting and the grave has lost its victory (1 Corinthians 15). Death for Adam, was a choice. Death was a self-inflicted, mortal wound upon mankind. **GOD DID NOT *KILL* ADAM AND EVE WITH DEATH** (as many teach). Rather, Adam and Eve died because of deliberate disobedience to God's Word by cutting themselves off from the life of God that comes only through obedience and dependence upon God's Word. Furthermore, in the Garden of Eden, we can see the significance of both Word and Sacrament through the prohibition that God places on the Tree of the Knowledge of Good and Evil. If you partake of that tree (the tree of the Knowledge of Good and Evil), you will surely die. That was not a threat, that was a promise – a fact! Conversely, the Tree of Life (not to be thought of as a "magic" tree, but) understood as the Divine sacramental tree and the source of immortality (a means of the grace which imparts continuing immortality). The Tree of Life was a type of Jesus in sacramental mystery. The book of Revelation makes this clear.

"He who has an ear, let him hear what the Spirit says to the churches. To the one who is victorious, I will grant the right to eat of the tree of life in the paradise of God" (Revelation 2:7 Berean). Fairbairn goes on to describe the Fall and what was lost by it. We were created to share in the divine life of God (the Holy Trinity), but that Divine life was lost when our first parents willfully disobeyed and forsook the life of love by declaring their independence from God's Word and thus were deceived by the Tempter's lie (Genesis chapter three). We should notice that faith and obedience always go hand in hand. Love and obedience also go hand in hand because "faith works by love." We obey God because we love God. If we don't obey God, we

don't love Him (John 14:15, 23). It's that simple! The effects of the Fall were devastating in that they are still seen and felt everywhere in creation to this very day. Therefore (as Paul says) "all creation groans for the manifestation of the sons of God" (Romans 8:22), a reality which will come to full fruition at Christ's Second Coming. The Parousia (Christ's Second Coming) will be a cosmic event which delivers all creation from the bondage of corruption. Until then, all creation still suffers the practical effects of The Fall and is subjection to corruption. Fairbairn highlights four ways this is so.

EFFECTS OF THE FALL:
(Source of Significance)

The primary effects of the adamic-fall are that mankind became slaves to a new law; the law of sin and death. *"For the law of the Spirit of life has set you free in Christ Jesus from the law of sin and death" (Romans 8:2).* Just to be clear at this point, the "law of sin and death" is not the Decalogue (i.e. The Ten Commandments). While it is true that The Decalogue defines sin (Romans 7:7) and it is true that the wages of sin is death (Romans 6:23). However, the law of God that defines sin is not the law of sin and death itself. God's law, The Ten Commandments are holy, just, good and spiritual (Romans 7:12). So now that we are clear on that point, what then is the "law of sin and death"? The "law of sin and death" is the habitual tendency (through inherited corruption in Adam) to sin (i.e. to transgress God's law: which includes The Ten Commandments). The work of regeneration through the infilling of the Holy Spirit, gives Believers the Divine power to live above our baser, primal, sinful tendency – not that we can become "sinless" in this present life, [81] but we can "sin-less." We are not espousing the heresy of "sinless perfection" in this life, but rather true holiness; without which no man will see the

Lord (Hebrews 12:14). I recently came across (source unknown) a supposedly Eastern Church definition of sin which I like.

> Sin is a terminal spiritual sickness which distorts the whole human being and corrupts the Image of God inherent in our human nature; diminishing the divine likeness within us, disorienting our understanding of the world around us, and distracting us from fulfilling our natural potential to experience communion with God.

I wish I could find the source of this quote because, in our opinion, it is accurate and worthy of further reflection. Donald Fairbairn [82] lists four subsequent effects of Adam's fall, which are adapted from his book "Life in the Trinity."

THE FIRST IS *SIGNIFICANCE*. Ever since the Fall, people have a misplaced sense of significance. Instead of finding our significance in the fact that we were created in God's image (which is something no other creature has – not even the angels), humans seek out significance in some connection to those people society says are significant (e.g. celebrities, athletes, etc.). Fairbairn states that there is nothing we need to "do" and indeed nothing that we can possibly "do" to find significance that would make us any more significant than we already are in God's sight JUST BECAUSE WE "ARE" His beloved creatures made *imago Dei*. As we shall see, this was the basic problem with the Prodigal Son, as evidenced in his "return home speech" in which he said: "I am no longer worthy to be called your son, make me as one of your hired servants." The Prodigal Son found his identity in his behavior rather than his belonging (to the father). His was a works mentality rather than a relational mentality. This is a primary problem even in the Body of Christ. Satan beats us up on our failed behavior and convinces us that we are no longer worthy and no longer loved of God. This could not be further from the truth. Our essential identity is based on who we are to God the Father, not on what we have done (or failed to do). Our significance is grounded in our being rather than our behavior. When this is understood – how amazing that our behavior automatically starts to line up with our identity. True love produces the fruit of repentance.

THE SECOND IS *PEACE*. Many moments in life are anxiety-producing. As human beings, we are fearful and troubled much of the time. Afraid of what? Afraid of wars, the safety of our loved ones, the troubles of this present life. Fears about the future, the unknown, you name it. Fairbairn contrasts these earthly fears with "the peace that passes all understanding" that Christ alone can give. The peace of Christ is NOT the elimination of the storm, but the promise of His abiding presence ("I will never leave you nor forsake you") during the storms of life. The promise that He will eventually calm the storms – but will even ride out the storms with us (He is in the boat with us). He gives us the Holy Spirit to remind us that there is an internal peace that does not depend on circumstances or even the elimination of the sources of stress or hostility, but rather depends on HIS ETERNAL PROMISES AND PERSONAL PRESENCE. The Prodigal Son had no peace. He had no peace because he was a "taker" and not a "giver". He had no peace because he was schismatic (departed from the household) and not a community builder. He had no peace because he focused on himself and not others. These are basic principles of God's kingdom which cannot be violated.

THE THIRD IS *WORK*. Fairbairn explains that our labor was originally intended to be a source of joy. The things we are working on are important to us; i.e. we feel a sense the importance of what we are doing. But work (in our fallen world) has become tedious and difficult and unsatisfying. But God in Christ through the abiding Holy Spirit – gives us something worth striving for: the spiritual food that comes from a relationship with Christ. We don't work "for" God – we work "from" (and through) God. Our labor is meant to be our delight. The word EDEN means "DELIGHT." The first habitat that God placed man was meant to be a place of delight (Psalm 16:11 "You make known to me the path of life; in your presence, there is fullness of joy; at your right hand are pleasures forevermore."). A relationship with Christ, Fairbairn says, is so liberating that it inspires us to work harder, but for different reasons. Working is not to find our significance – but because we get to create (recreate) with God for the sheer joy of being co-creators (in a limited sense) with God Himself. How interesting that the Prodigal Son forsook the work of the family farm and wasted his inheritance until we again found himself working – but this time in the pig pen. Work was a drudgery. Work was a curse in this environment (to him) because he was not serving a proper cause. He was just trying to survive. God has called us to thrive and not just survive!

THE FOURTH IS *RELATIONSHIP*. Sin has caused us to manipulate one another; to use and abuse one another for selfish gain. Appropriate relationships are only possible when we experience mutual submission out of love and serving one another in love. Relationships at home, in school, at work, are to seen as a privilege and not a competition or drudgery. Human relationships are a way of reflecting something of God's own inter-Trinitarian nature in our everyday lives. *"Whatever we do, whether we eat or drink, we do all to the glory of God."* Even a "cup of cold water" given in a prophet's name receives a prophet's reward. There is no such thing as insignificant activity. We were meant to live in the LOVE, JOY and PEACE of God. The Elder Brother Syndrome represents the Pharisee spirit. Jesus was all about restored fellowship as modeled by the father's response. It is unfortunate that over the centuries this parable has become known as that of the Prodigal Son, because it is the father who is the true centerpiece of the story, flanked as he is on either side by his two very different sons." [83]

STUDY QUESTIONS (PART-1):

From: *THE DIVINE IMPERATIVE:*

1. What is the center of Christian worship?
2. What does the word "Eucharist" mean?
3. Comment on the "imperative of the father" in light of the Eucharist.
4. List 5-things that are already true of us "in Christ" from Ephesians chapter 1.
5. Albert Schweitzer called "being in Christ" the (what – fill in the blank)?

From: *THE JOY OF THE LORD:*

6. Explain in your own words, what St. Isaac the Syrian meant by: "Our compassionate Creator is not overcome by the wickedness of His creatures"?
7. What does the author mean: "God is not a lonely monad"?
8. To say that "God is love" means that God is (fill in the blank)?

From: *THE DANCE OF GOD:*

9. What does "perichoresis" mean? Break down the two parts of the word.
10. How does Douglas Kelly explain perichoresis?

From: *INTIMATE FELLOWSHIP:*

11. What did John mean in John 1:18 when he said that the Son has ever-lived in the "bosom of the father"?
12. Love requires 3 things. List them.

13. Describe each member of the Trinity in relation to these three things (see above question).
14. The life of the Trinity is characterized not by self-centeredness but by (fill in the blank).

From: *LIFE IN THE TRINITY:*

15. It is from a sense of (fill in the blank) that true inner transformation may safely occur.
16. What is the reason for the incarnation?
17. What does the word "philosophy" mean?
18. What is Christianity at its core?
19. Why does God find delight in us?
20. The truest thing about us is (fill in the blank)?

From: *FACE TO FACE WITH GOD:*

21. We become "sons of God" (fill in the blank) because of who we are (fill in the blank).

From: *HIS IDENTITY AND OURS:*

22. St. Athanasius (4th century) said… "He (Christ) became what we are that we might (fill in the blank)?

From: *NEW CREATION IN CHRIST:*

23. Repentance cannot remedy fallen nature: we are corrupted and need to be (fill in the blank)?
24. What is meant by the statement: "Jesus relived Adam's life backwards; for us/as us, and rebooted the human-race"?

KNOWING THE FATHER'S HEART

From: *GOD'S ESSENTIAL NATURE:*

25. The essence of who God is in eternity and in redemptive history is contained in the phrase (fill in the blank)?
26. What did St. Teresa of Avila say about love?
27. What does the "kenosis" mean?

From: *THROUGH THE LOOKING-GLASS:*

28. What does the author mean by saying that "Jesus came into the world to reveal the 'upside-down' kingdom?

From the next two sections:

29. List the seven-fold emptying of Christ.
30. List the seven-fold exaltation of Christ.

From: *LOVE, GLORY AND ELECTION:*

31. Gregory of Palamas, said that "God does not decide what men's will shall be. It is not that He (fill in the blank) and thus foreknows, but that He (fill in the blank) and thus foreordains.
32. Karl Barth said that "Jesus Christ is the electing God and (fill in the blank) in One.
33. Explain this statement: "Hell is the unbeliever's unreality into eternity."
34. What does C.S. Lewis call "the painful refuge"? Explain.
35. Compare Jonah 4:2 with Exodus 33:19

From: *THE PRIMARY DOCTRINE:*

36. What were the first four ecumenical councils about essentially?

KNOWING THE FATHER'S HEART

37. According to Donald Fairbairn, why does the contemporary church often regard theology/doctrine as somewhat irrelevant to the Christian life?
38. We need to study God to know God as He is, and not just (fill in the blank)?

From: *MONARCHY OF THE FATHER:*

39. What is the primary difference between mankind and the rest of creation?
40. According to Matthew 11:27, Jesus is the only one who declares (fill in the blank).
41. Death is essentially what (fill in the blank)?
42. The Parousia will be a cosmic event which does what (fill in the blank)?

From: *THE EFFECTS OF THE FALL:*

43. According to the Eastern Church, sin is a (fill in the blank) which distorts the whole (fill in the blank) and corrupts the (fill in the blank) inherent in our nature; diminishing the (fill in the blank) within us and disorienting our (fill in the blank) and distracting us from (fill in the blank).
44. From the endnotes (#71), what was A.J. Gordon's quote in contrasting the twin heresies of "sinless perfection" with "sinful imperfection"? Explain briefly.

~ *Knowing the Father's Heart (Part 2)* ~
PRACTICAL IMPLICATIONS OF LOVE

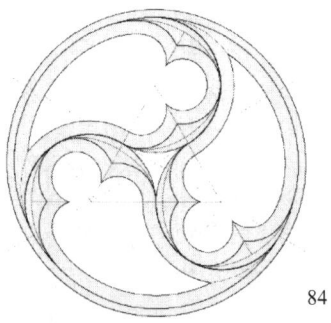

84

A PARABLE IS...
(Earthly story, Heavenly meaning)

"The truths of the Gospel come to us in a variety of ways. One way is through Jesus' favorite teaching method: 'PARABLES.' "As a translation of the Hebrew word מָשָׁל mashal, the word "parable" can also refer to a riddle." "The use of parables by Jesus was hence a natural teaching method that fit into the tradition of his time." [85] By some estimates, there are as many as forty-six [86] parables in the New Testament Gospels. Parables are a means of communicating spiritual truths using familiar earthly things, and their overall focus in the Kingdom." [87] Another way of explaining a parable is a simple story used to illustrate a spiritual lesson related to God's rule and reign on earth. Parable telling was Jesus' favorite form of teaching to the multitudes. Some have called parables "earthly stories with heavenly meaning." In Matthew chapter thirteen, Jesus explains why He spoke in parables (i.e. His motivation for telling parables). Jesus mostly taught the multitudes in parables. Jesus was the consummate story-teller. Furthermore (and this may sound incredible), but parable telling (especially in the case of Jesus) had a two-fold purpose in His ministry: (a) to clarify the truth to the sincere, and (b) to conceal the truth from the insincere. Jesus said the following words:

> Because it has been given to you to know the mysteries of the kingdom of heaven, but to them it has not been given... And in them the prophecy of Isaiah is fulfilled, which says: 'Hearing you will hear and shall not understand, and seeing you will see and not perceive, for the heart of this people has grown dull. Their ears are hard of hearing, and their eyes they have closed, lest they should see with their eyes and hear with their ears, lest they should understand with their heart and turn, so that I should heal them (Matthew 13:11,14,15).

One more thing. Parables were meant to deeply disturb (if need be) the recalcitrant heart. With that background, let us consider the parable of the Prodigal Son (so called). In the case of the Prodigal Son parable, it had a most compelling back-story which helps us understand something of God's essential nature and character. As we have explained in the first part of this study guide, the parable of the prodigal son is the third in a trio of parables told by Christ in Luke chapter fifteen. Notice how the percentages diminish in each one.

- The first parable in this chapter had 1 of 100 (only 1%) becoming lost (i.e. the parable of the lost sheep).
- The second parable had 1 of 10 (10%) becoming lost.
- The third parable (the prodigal son) had 1 of 2 (50%) becoming lost.

This diminishing sequence emphasizes the magnitude of the loss to the father in the lost son. Jesus did this to great effect in order to build the suspense. To lose half your sons would be a great tragedy and likewise, to regain half your sons would be cause for great rejoicing. However, the real point here is not the percentages. The real point here is that God cares for ALL THE LOST, the last and the least! With that introduction, now let us examine the third parable in greater detail as the primary subject of our inquiry.

THERE WAS A MAN
(God's heart in a metaphor)

"There was a man." Here we find a standard introduction; not an uncommon way to begin a story in antiquity, especially to Biblically Literate Jewish people of Jesus' day. "Jewish people in Jesus' day would be naturally inclined to identify with the younger son, knowing well the stories of Cain and Abel, Isaac and Ishmael, and Jacob and Esau. But to our surprise, in this parable, the younger son turns out not to be the righteous Abel, or the faithful Isaac, or even the clever Jacob, but rather he turns out to be an irresponsible, self-indulgent child." [88] The story speaks of "the younger son." Since there is no mention of a wife, it is likely that he was in his late teens or early twenties. We should become acquainted with the social fabric of family life in the ancient Jewish world (and the following background is readily available from a number of reliable sources).

> When the father divided the property between his two sons, and the younger son turned his share of the inheritance into cash. This probably meant that the land owned by the father, had been split into two, with the younger son selling off his share to someone else (an unknown third party). Normally, firstborn sons were given twice as much as other sons (a.k.a. the double

portion blessing). We do not know if this was always done in Jesus' day. If so, the younger son would have received one third of the estate. The specific amount of the inheritance isn't stressed in the story, nor are we told how the property was divided because such details are not the point of the story. [89] [90]

The point of the story is fellowship lost and regained; broken and restored. This is the point of the parable because this is the point of redemptive history itself. This is the point of the Bible. The Bible is essentially "God's-story" (HIStory). It's all about God in relationship with mankind. It's God's redemption-story! In looking at this parable, we immediately see the selfishness and shamefulness of the prodigal son in demanding an early inheritance while the father was yet alive. It was unthinkable that a son would demand such before his father's death. It was a deeply dishonoring demand! When the younger son said *give me,* it was like saying: I can't wait around here any longer. I wish you were dead.

> He was not just asking for his inheritance, which is normally divided after the father dies, he was basically telling his father to drop dead, I am done with you and I'm outta here. He went to a "far country" meaning that he wanted to get as far away from his father (God) as possible. [91]

Obviously, this was a clear violation of the fifth commandment; *"Honor your father and your mother."* Interestingly, that is the only Biblical command (of the Ten Commandments) that has a PROMISE attached with it (according to Ephesians 6:3: "that it may be well with you, and you may live long on the earth"). Again – God is all about relationship because God is relationship; Father, Son and Spirit. This gets to the heart of reality. This is more than just a

Christian or Jewish religious thing – this is the reality of life itself. The younger son was denying this most essential thing about life itself. To him – relationships didn't matter much. The younger son treated his father as if he were dead. In so doing, he violated his father's honor, but revealed the extent of his self-centeredness – which is the very definition of sin. This gets to the heart of *The Fall* of man in the garden – man's declaration of independence from God always results in his alienation from his fellow man. Sadly, this is also the point of man-made religion (to use the word "religion" in its negative context). It is all about the rules, whereas *true* religion (to use the word "religion" in its positive context) is all about relationship! *"Pure and undefiled religion in the sight of our God and Father is this: to visit orphans and widows in their distress, and to keep oneself unstained by the world" (James 1:27 NASB).* The younger son's underlying motivation was self-serving (i.e. 'what's in it for me').

Everyone's favorite radio station is: W.I.I.F.M. (what's in it for me). The prodigal had little thought or desire for community. He didn't care what his actions meant for others. *Empathy* (the noun) means: "the ability to understand and share the feelings of another." In the extreme, a *sociopath* is someone without an ability to understand or share the feelings of others. Life is always about relationships. Sin is essentially a failure in relationship. Sin is more than a moral infraction. The law of love is always behind God's moral law. God's moral law is simply a reflection of His moral character. The laws of God therefore are all the things that love DOES and DOESN'T do. For this reason, Jesus said that to love God and your neighbor is a fulfillment of all the law and the prophets.

> Jesus replied: "'Love the Lord your God with all your heart and with all your soul and with all your mind.' This is the first and greatest commandment. And the second is like it: 'Love your neighbor as yourself.' All the Law

and the Prophets hang on these two commandments." (Matthew 22:37-40).

Just to be clear, sin is a transgression of the law of God. But it goes deeper than that. SIN IS TRANSGRESSION AGAINST LOVE. With God, it's more personal and relational than legal. Sin is the transgression of the law – yes. But more than that, sin is the transgression of love and relationship. Another word in the family of love-language words is "compassion." Throughout the Gospels, can see that Jesus was always "moved with compassion" and did something. COMPASSION IS LOVE MOVED TO ACTION. Jesus is the human face of the incarnate God. Jesus is the love of God manifest to mankind in the flesh. Jesus is God with "skin" on (if you will). God the Son became incarnate in time, space, history to show us the love of God in all its perfect clarity and absolute purity. As T.F. Torrance said: "there is no God behind the back of Jesus Christ." [92] Jesus is the only human face of God. The Father and the Son do not share a different point of view. Not only does Jesus love you, but the Father Himself loves you (says our Lord Jesus in the Gospel of John 16:27). There is Trinitarian solidarity within the Godhead. God is love ontologically (i.e. in the nature of His being) as well as in the economy of salvation. The reason why God in Christ was so *"moved with compassion"* (compassion being defined as "love expressed to human need") is because God is love from all eternity; before time, space, and history itself. When love became incarnate in Christ, He was the fullest measure of compassionate love.

- (Mark 1:40-41) "A man with leprosy came to him and begged him on his knees, "If you are willing, you can make me clean. Filled with compassion, Jesus reached out his hand and touched the man. 'I am willing,' he said. 'Be clean!'"

- (Mark 6:34) "When Jesus landed and saw a large crowd, he had compassion on them, because they were like sheep without a shepherd. So, he began teaching them many things."
- (Mark 8:2) "I have compassion for these people; they have already been with me three days and have nothing to eat."
- (Matthew 9:36) "When he saw the crowds, he had compassion on them, because they were harassed and helpless, like sheep without a shepherd."
- (Matthew 14:14) "When Jesus landed and saw a large crowd, he had compassion on them and healed their sick."
- (Luke 15:20) "So he got up and went to his father. 'But while he was still a long way off, his father saw him and was filled with compassion for him; he ran to his son, threw his arms around him and kissed him.'"
- (Matthew 20:34) "Jesus had compassion on them and touched their eyes. Immediately they received their sight and followed him."

The prodigal son, in contrast to Jesus, had little regard for others. He paid no apparent regard to his father's reputation in the village or the family name. He despised his birthright and blessing as Esau did before him (Genesis 25:29-34; Hebrews 12:16). The prodigal son had no desire for the "household of God" (the "Qahal" – in the Hebrew language, the "Ekklesia" – in the Greek language). This attitude runs contrary to the Divine motivation and logic of creation.

> Apart from love nothing whatever has existed, nor ever will. Its names and actions are many. More numerous still are its distinctive marks; divine and innumerable are

its properties. Yet it is one in nature, wholly beyond utterance whether on the part of angels or men or any other creatures, even such as are unknown to us. Reason cannot comprehend it; its glory is inaccessible, its counsels unsearchable. It is eternal because it is beyond time, invisible because thought cannot comprehend it, though it may perceive it. Many are the beauties of this holy Sion not made with hands! He who has begun to see it no longer delights in sensible objects; he ceases to be attached to the glory of this world. [93] ~ St. Symeon the New Theologian.

FATHER'S APPARENT INACTION:
(Why God allows it)

Let us now consider the apparent inaction of the father in response to the selfish demand of his son. It may appear that the father failed to discipline his son. The father may appear to be complicit in the rebellious son's debauchery. But such is not the case; and this gets to the heart of the mystery of iniquity itself (the problem of evil). The truth is that the apparent inaction of the father reveals a deeper and more profound revelation (a twin-revelation) concerning love. The apparent inaction of the father reveals: (a) who we are as human beings, and (b) who God is in His triune nature. To the first point, we (as humans) have what I like to call "frightful freedom." We are free moral agents to such a degree that it is "frightful" if we stop and think about it. Moral choice is part and parcel to being created *imago Dei* (Genesis 1:27). Our choices are real! Our choices have consequences! To the second point, GOD IS LOVE (1 John 4:8, 16) and LOVE IS ALWAYS A CHOICE! Love must be free (Matthew 10:8). In my opinion, this is the reason for the "mystery of iniquity" (2 Thessalonians 2:7) (a.k.a. the problem of evil; as it is often called in theological circles). This point is important! The abysmal irrationality of evil in our world can only be explained by the freedom that love demands (because God is love) to facilitate authentic fellowship and communion. For love to be legitimately experienced, it's negation must be permitted. This is the best explanation for the existence of evil in the universe, in my opinion. However unreasonable and absurd it is for free moral agents to turn away from a loving God – personal freedom makes it possible because love is always a choice and therefore its negation (its refusal) creates the opposite; the pseudo world of un-love (evil). Whenever God gives a command, He also gives the power to obey that command. All decisions to obey God's Word are empowered by God. If God commands that we love one another (and He does), then we can do it. If God commands it, we can do it! God's love working in us can cause us to do as He does. It's our choice, but it's His power. We can do all things through Christ which strengthens us! Even the most difficult things. I am reminded of the intense suffering and persecution for the faith endured by St. Maximus the Confessor – who dared to stand up for the truth of the Gospel. Love is always a choice.

> "But I say to you," the Lord says, "love your enemies, do good to those who hate you, pray for those who persecute you." Why did he command these things? So that he might free us from hatred, sadness, anger and grudges, and might grant us the greatest possession of all, perfect love, which is impossible to possess except by the one who loves all equally in imitation of God. (~ St. Maximus the Confessor). [94]

JESUS IS GOD FROM GOD
(No God behind the back of Jesus Christ!)

Jesus is not only the coming of God in the flesh; Immanuel, but He is the "new Adam," the "new mankind," the "new creation," man of very man. Jesus is both the face of God to man and the face of man (man as we were supposed to be in the presence of God). As previously stated, Professor Torrance was fond of saying: "there is no other God behind the back of Jesus," [95] meaning: Jesus is not merely "like" God, but He "is" God from God, light from light, true God from true God. God has no hidden decree (election) behind the back of Jesus. If we are chosen and loved in Christ, we are chosen and loved of the Father. That's the point! John 1:1 says, *"In the beginning was the Word, and the Word was with God, and the Word was God."* [96] Jesus is the image of God; God from God, begotten from His eternal nature.

> God, who at various times and in various ways spoke in time past to the fathers by the prophets, has in these last days spoken to us by His Son, whom He has appointed heir of all things, through whom also He made the worlds; who being the brightness of His glory and the express image of His person, and upholding all things by the word of His power, when He had by Himself purged our sins, sat down at the right hand of the Majesty on high. (Hebrews 1:1-3 NKJV).

To elaborate, the evangelical truth: *"there is no God behind the back of Jesus Christ"* was firmly impressed upon the young mind of Torrance during his military service in World War II as a chaplain in the British army. After an engagement in Italy, Torrance went in search of wounded soldiers:

When daylight filtered through I came across a young soldier (private Phillips) scarcely twenty years old lying mortally wounded on the ground, who clearly had not long to live. As I knelt and bent over him, he said "Padre, is God really like Jesus?" I assured him that he was ... As I prayed and commended him to the Lord Jesus he passed away. [97]

When we die (and everyone will one day die: "... its appointed unto every man once to die and after that the judgment" [Hebrews 9:27]), we will discover that God the Son is God from God! This is fundamental to our Christian faith and not a peripheral issue! It's a matter of life and death. Jesus is not different in nature than God the Father. In theological terms, the *homoousion* [98] of the Council of Nicaea [99] boldly declared the ontological identity of Jesus Christ with the Creator of the universe. The result was that this definition and clarity produced the most important creed in Christian history: The Nicene Creed. [100]

THE NICENE CREED:
(Universal confession of the Church)

"The Nicene Creed is the only authoritative ecumenical statement of the Christian faith accepted by the Roman Catholic, Eastern Orthodox, Oriental Orthodox, Anglican, and the major Protestant denominations" in Christendom. [101] It is considered likely that this creed was adopted at the 381 Second Ecumenical Council (First Council of Constantinople). [102]

I BELIEVE in one God the Father Almighty, Maker of heaven and earth, And of all things visible and invisible: And in one Lord Jesus Christ, the only-begotten Son of God; Begotten of his Father before all worlds, God of God, Light of Light, Very God of very God; Begotten, not made; Being of one substance with the Father; By whom all things were made: Who for us men and for our salvation came down from heaven, And was incarnate by the Holy Ghost of the Virgin Mary, And was made man: And was crucified also for us under Pontius Pilate; He suffered and was buried: And the third day he rose again according to the Scriptures: And ascended into heaven, And sitteth on the right hand of the Father: And he shall come again, with glory, to judge both the quick and the dead; Whose kingdom shall have no end. And I believe in the Holy Ghost, The Lord, and Giver of Life, Who proceedeth from the Father and the Son; Who with the Father and the Son together is worshipped and glorified;

Who spake by the Prophets: And I believe one Catholic and Apostolic Church: I acknowledge one Baptism for the remission of sins: And I look for the Resurrection of the dead: And the Life of the world to come. Amen.

During the fourth century, Arians and Semi-Arians were content to affirm the "likeness" of Jesus Christ to the Father. They disagree about the points of likeness; but they all agreed that there could not be an identity of being. In their eyes, such an assertion would compromise the simplicity and transcendence of God. In their understanding, the Son was a creature; created by the unbegotten God from out of nothing. No matter how exalted a creature He may be, the distance between the Son and his Maker is infinite. "The one thing that the Arian Christ cannot communicate to humanity is God." [104] To the Arians, it was blasphemy to say that Jesus "is" God from God. The modern-day equivalent of Arianism is the "Jehovah's Witnesses" sect; the Watchtower Bible and Tract Society. In fact, fourth century Arianism (which nearly split the entire Christian church) was not as dangerous as modern day Jehovah's Witness doctrine because at least Arius (4th century) believed that Jesus should be worshipped – whereas the Jehovah's Witnesses teach that since one is to worship God alone, therefore Jesus should not be worshipped because he is merely a creature. Fr. George D. Dragas said the following: "if Jesus of Nazareth reveals God, then He must be really God, and if He is really God, He must be God the Creator. There is no incompatibility or opposition between the uncreated and the created. God is uncreated in the Father, but He is Creator in the Son." [105] This is the primary difference between the heretic Arius and the great doctor of the church; St Athanasius, concerning the doctrine of Christ. T.F. Torrance explains: "the fact that God himself, God incarnate, penetrated into our damned existence and death in order to save us, reveals the bottomless chasm and the irrational, inexplicable nature of evil by which we are separated from him." [106]

> Perhaps the most fundamental truth which we must learn in the Christian Church, or rather relearn since we have suppressed it, is that the incarnation was the coming of God to save us in the heart of our fallen and depraved humanity, where humanity is at its wickedest in its enmity and violence against the reconciling love of God. That is to say, the incarnation is to be understood as the coming of God to take upon Himself our fallen human nature, our actual human existence laden with sin and guilt, our humanity diseased in mind and soul in its estrangement or alienation from the Creator. [107]

Jesus joined Adam (as it were) behind the tree in the Garden of Eden (this side of the fall), and by His perfect obedience (Jesus did no sin, He had no sin, no guile was found in His mouth), Jesus bent the human will back to God for us and as us one Nano-moment at a time. This is the deeper meaning of the incarnation. This is how Christ (and Christ alone) brought about a new creation – for only He could accomplish it. He perfectly represented both God to man (God of very God) and man to God (the new creation, faithful Israel, the last Adam) and thus our perfect mediator. Another way of looking at this parable might be to say that Jesus became (as it were) the prodigal son (He came in our place and for our benefit). By His incarnation, Jesus went into the far country of our lost condition and brought us back home through His vicarious obedience; safe into the father's embrace. That is the basic story within the story. But before we go further down that road, let us not forget the surface meaning of the parable as we attempt to unpack its deeper meaning.

INTO A FAR COUNTRY:
(Man's sad exile)

The parable of the prodigal son reads like the story of Israel in their abandonment of God's covenant promises and commands. But it also reads like the history of all humanity (in the Garden of Eden). In Genesis chapter three – we read that the sin of Adam and Eve led to their exile from the Garden. In the parable of the prodigal son, we find a similar situation. As the story goes, without much of any warning, the prodigal son cuts himself off from his family, his friends, his neighbors, his homeland, and heads off to a far country. He makes his way into (what would have been considered in the eyes of good Jewish people) unclean gentile territory. Again, to the original listeners of this parable – the actions of the young prodigal would have primarily represented the actions of rebellious "Israel" (as a nation) who had gone into forced exile some 500-years prior because of their stubborn disobedience to God and idolatry. The parallels here are unmistakable! N.T. Wright and the new perspective on Paul, represents a significant shift in the way some scholars, especially Protestant scholars, interpret the writings of the Apostle Paul. What does this have to do with the Prodigal Son? Everything! The problem with the prodigal was not simply that he had personally "sinned" and needed to be "justified" (saved) – that is also true. But the problem with the prodigal son was that he represented the state of Israel as a nation (a chosen people) in exile from God without realizing that in Christ, God the Father Himself was standing in their very midst with arms open ready to welcome them back home, if only they would return the hug. The parable had a collective application that Israel failed to realize. This essential truth was not appreciated by the majority of the people to whom the Gospel was first preached (except for the Jewish remnant). According to N.T. Wright, "justification" is not the center of

Paul's thought (this harkens back to the first part of this study guide), but rather the outworking of it. The following quote may help to clarify this statement.

> The doctrine of justification by faith is not what Paul means by 'the gospel'. It is implied by the gospel; when the gospel is proclaimed, people come to faith and so are regarded by God as members of his people. But 'the gospel' is not an account of how people get saved. It is, as we saw in an earlier chapter, the proclamation of the lordship of Jesus Christ... Let us be quite clear. 'The gospel' is the announcement of Jesus' lordship, which works with power to bring people into the family of Abraham, now redefined around Jesus Christ and characterized solely by faith in him. 'Justification' is the doctrine which insists that all those who have this faith belong as full members of this family, on this basis and no other. [108]

The parallels between the prodigal son and apostate Israel in exile should have been obvious to the original hearers. They have equally ominous warnings for the contemporary church. The essential definition of apostasy is to "stray from the faith" (i.e. to forsake the way of truth and life, and to do so willingly and wantonly). Paul warned, *"The Spirit clearly says that in later times some will abandon the faith and follow deceiving spirits and things taught by demons" (1 Timothy 4:1).* As the prodigal left the loving and gracious house of his father, he traveled into a far county where the "love of strangers" was not in the law code. Remember, the law of Moses required God's people to love the stranger, the orphan, the oppressed. But here again, the prodigal, instead of showing reckless generosity, wastes all his inheritance and scatters his property; squandering his wealth in dissolute living. At this point we should notice that the details of the sins were intentionally left out of the story. Why? Because they are not the real point of the story. Jesus was NOT chronicling the transgressions of the prodigal (as the Pharisees would have done if they were telling the story). The prodigal's sins were as deplorable as they were many. We don't make light of that fact! However, the sins of the prodigal did not change the heart of the father towards his lost son. The actions of the father in this parable represent the heart of our heavenly Father. Consider the following...

O HAPPY FAULT
(Understanding The Fall):

Sometimes we fail to view *Adam's Fall* through the eyes of Divine providence. The Fall of man – and by consequence, the fall of creation – did not take God by surprise. The Church Fathers thought much and wrote often of this now forgotten concept. Consider the Latin expression: *felix culpa.* This phrase was made popular in the writings of St. Augustine (4th century) as the source of Original Sin because of *The Fall* in the Garden. Augustine said:

> *Melius enim iudicavit de malis benefacere, quam mala nulla esse permittere* (being interpreted): *"For God judged it better to bring good out of evil than not to permit any evil to exist."* [109]

Felix culpa comes from the Latin words *felix* (meaning 'happy,' 'lucky,' or 'blesse') and *culpa* (meaning 'fault' or 'fall'); most often translated 'happy fault.' The Catholic Paschal Vigil Mass states: *Exsultet O felix culpa quae talem et tantum meruit habere redemptorem,* which by translation means: *"O happy fault that earned for us so great, so glorious a Redeemer."*

Felix culpa, as a theological construct, probably originated not from St. Augustine of Hippo (4th century) however, but from his theological mentor; St. Ambrose of Milan (4th century). Ambrose spoke of the <u>fortunate ruin</u> of Adam in the Garden of Eden in such a way that Adam's sin brought more-good to humanity than if Adam had remained perfectly innocent. This line of thought became the basic theodicy of the patristic and medieval church.

> The medieval theologian; Thomas Aquinas (13th century) cited this line when he explained how the principle that "God allows evils to happen in order to bring a greater good therefrom" underlies the causal relation between original sin and the Divine Redeemer's Incarnation, thus concluding that a higher state is not inhibited by sin. [110]

The *Felix culpa* concept is also found in the Hebrew/Jewish tradition in *The Exodus* from Egypt where it is associated with God's judgment. Although *The Exodus* is not a fall (per se), the thinking goes that without the wilderness exile, the people of God would not have enjoyed finding the Promised Land. Through trial and suffering came the hope of victory and restored life. [111] In modern literature, the *Felix culpa* is described as a series of unfortunate events which eventually lead to a happier outcome, as depicted in Raphael Carter's 1996 science fiction novel entitled: "The Fortunate Fall." This takes us back to the parable once again.

LOST BUT VALUABLE:
(Intrinsic value in God's sight)

> *"How deep the Father's love for us, how vast beyond all measure That He should give His Only Son, to make a wretch His treasure"* ~ by Stuart Townend

The primary theme of the parable of the prodigal son is the revelation of the father's love and grace. Notice how the text reads... *"he (the prodigal) spent everything... and began to be in need."* The boy's poverty is emphasized *("he began to be in need")* rather than the obvious deficiencies in his character. Jesus placed the primary emphasis on the boy's LOST CONDITION rather than his GUILT. This is important! Was the prodigal son guilty? Yes. Absolutely! But was that the point of the story? No! God sees all sinners as lost (which also means that they are guilty, but that is not the point here). When Jesus spoke of the lost sheep, or the lost coin, or the lost son – He was emphasizing their worth (i.e. worthy of being found, saved, delivered). When something is lost, it is worthy of being found because it has a home, it has an owner. It isn't worthless, it doesn't just go missing. It is lost; meaning, it has value to the owner. This was scandalous theology to ears of the first century religious class (the Pharisees).

Pharisee-ism was/is a works-based religion and not a grace-based revelation (the true revelation of Scripture). This was the constant challenge of Jesus throughout His earthly ministry. He (personally) is the way, the truth and the life. He didn't come to merely show us the way or the truth – He is the very embodiment of truth and life and desires to share it with us. All mankind has intrinsic value in the eyes of God. When we consider once again the fact that humanity (without Christ) is lost, that does not mean "rejected." It means exactly the opposite. When someone or something is "lost," it has intrinsic value/worth in the eyes of the beholder. God places great value on every human being created in the likeness of God. Sin doesn't change that fact. We are not suggesting that God loves sin (God in fact hates "sin"). Don't be confused at this point. However, God loves sinners *("of whom I am the chief"* – said Paul). God hates sins but loves the sinner! This is the balanced understanding of this power principle. Jesus said... *"I have not come to call the righteous, but sinners to repentance" (Luke 5:32). "But go and learn what this means: 'I desire mercy, not sacrifice.' For I have not come to call the righteous, but sinners" (Matthew 9:13).* Paul said... *"But God demonstrates his own love for us in this: While we were still sinners, Christ died for us (Romans 5:8 NIV).*

UNDERSTANDING LOVE-WRATH:
(God is not bi-polar!)

The truth expressed in the last section has been clouded and all but lost in some circles (how ironic that the meaning of "lostness" has been "lost"). This has especially been the case in some Protestant circles, especially since the enlightenment. This was never more true than in the case of the 18th century America puritan preaching of the venerable Jonathan Edwards. Historian Perry Miller suggests that America's Enlightenment began and ended with Jonathan Edwards. Edwards played a defining role in bridging the space between Puritanism and what would eventually become American evangelicalism. I do not wish to sharpen the point too much here considering the many good things that could be said about the ministry of eminent puritan theologian; Jonathan Edwards. I am not an Edwards scholar, but as good Edwards was for the "Great American Awakening," he did not appear to have a balanced view of God's love. It would appear to me that Edwards was confused about the nature of God's love; considering that he wrote conflicting concepts in "Sinners in the hands of an angry God" [112] (his most famous sermon) and "Love, the sum of all virtue." [113] Edwards rightly discerned that "all the virtue that is saving and that distinguishes true Christians from others, is summed up in Christian love." [114] But consider in his own words, the following lines from his most famous sermon: *"Sinners in the hands of an angry God."*

The God that holds you over the pit of Hell, much as one holds a spider, or some loathsome insect, over the fire, abhors you, and is dreadfully provoked; his wrath towards you burns like fire; he looks upon you as worthy of nothing else, but to be cast into the fire; he is of purer eyes than to bear to have you in his sight; you are ten thousand times so abominable in his eyes as the most hateful venomous serpent is in ours. You have offended him infinitely more than ever a stubborn rebel did his prince: and yet 'tis nothing but his hand that holds you from falling into the fire every moment: 'tis to be ascribed to nothing else, that you did not go to Hell the last night... but that God's hand has held you up: there is no other reason to be given why you haven't gone to Hell since you have sat here in the house of God, provoking his pure eyes by your sinful wicked manner of attending his solemn worship: yea, there is nothing else that is to be given as a reason why you don't this very moment drop down into Hell. Oh, sinner! Consider the fearful danger you are in."

What should we make of this terrifying presentation, even if the rhetoric was intended for maximum shock value to compel sinners to repent? While it appears that God's grace and love are throughout Edwards other sermons and writings, the assertion here that God *'abhors you'* is heterodox. This kind of *bipolar presentation* has caused much confusion within American Protestant Christianity.

Puritans like Jonathan Edwards believed that one must first experience God's wrath in order to be reborn of God's grace. Regrettable as his rhetoric is, Edwards really did hope his hearers would then experience God's grace. From an Orthodox point of view, this is wrongheaded in divorcing regeneration from baptism.

He also fails, however, to see the unity of these two in the light of divine love, coming down far too heavy-handedly.[115]

Undoubtedly, Edwards believed (as many do today) that God *abhors us* before He *loves us*. It seems that many Christians can't figure out whether: "He loves me, or He loves me not." This is what a lopsided presentation of the Gospel will do. Some wonder if God (the Father) is love, or perhaps only Jesus (the Son), or if perhaps God is both loving and unloving (something like the "Star Wars" series). Perhaps God has a dark/ominous side. The confusion goes on and on. In "Star Wars," the force is comprised of both the light and the dark side. Such an idol-god image is patently false, and yet I would bet that many Christians believe it today. The truth of The Gospel is this: (A) God hates sin and His wrath against evil is real. (B) God's love for people and His wrath against sin are not to be understood as two opposite, contradictory things. Rather, they are the two sides of His loving nature (like heads and tails). In other words, because God is love, He is just. Conversely, because God is just, He is love. Both are true at the same time. But they are not two different things. They are one in the same point. Think of it this way: when sin and evil is exposed to God's love – judgement/wrath occurs. God's love is <u>not</u> antithetical to His wrath. Rather, God's wrath is a byproduct of His love; demanding it. If God were not just, He would not be love. In the words of St. Maximus, the Confessor (7th century):

> God, it is said, is the Sun of righteousness (cf. Malachi 4:2), and the rays of His supernal goodness shine down on all men alike. The soul is wax if it cleaves to God, but clay if it cleaves to matter. Which it does depends upon its own will and purpose. Clay hardens in the sun, while wax grows soft. Similarly, every soul that, despite God's admonitions, deliberately cleaves to the material world, hardens like clay and drives itself to destruction, just as

Pharaoh did (cf. Exodus 7:13). But every soul that cleaves to God is softened like wax and, receiving the impress and stamp of divine realities, it becomes "in spirit the dwelling-place of God" (Ephesians 2:22). [116]

The hinge, according to St. Maximus, is our own disposition. Remove the warmth of the sun and neither will wax soften nor will clay harden. In both cases, the reality behind the experience of grace and the experience of wrath is really one and the same: "the rays of [God's] supernal goodness." As Vladimir Lossky put it, "At the second coming of Christ... the love of God will be an intolerable torment for those who have not acquired it within themselves." [117]

In our opinion, St. Maximus expressed accurately the heart of God on this matter. St. Ambrose of Milan (4th century) wrote, *"The wicked man is a punishment to himself, but the upright man is a grace to himself—and to either, whether good or bad, the reward of his deeds is paid in his own person."* C.S. Lewis (20th century) wrote this in "The Great Divorce," *"At the end of all things... the Blessed will say, 'We have never lived anywhere except in Heaven,' and the Lost, 'We were always in Hell.' And both will speak truly."* What Lewis means here is that our choices are real and that God honors them; not because He is capricious, but because He is love and that is the nature of love.

The bottom line is this – the wrath and love of God are not 'separate energies' from God; one sent to punish sin and the other to reward evil. Rather, they are reactions when the human soul encounters the uncreated energies of God. Someone who embraces sin will react on contact with the experience of wrath, something like gasoline when exposed to fire – whereas someone walking in the Holy Spirit and obedience to God will experience love and grace. Put another way; through sin we make ourselves 'allergic' to divine grace and susceptible to divine wrath, whereas through obedience to God's word and sacraments, we rid ourselves of this 'allergy.' [118]

LOVE MUST BE FREE!
(Whosoever will may come)

Paulo Coelho said: *"If you love someone, you must be prepared to set them free"*. Returning to the parable itself, we notice that the father allowed his younger son to go into the far country. The point being that LOVE MUST BE FREE! Even if the father would have pursued him – the prodigal would have strayed even further into a more distance country. In this, we find two principles: (1) God only pursues us (in our straying) when we are lost and do not know the way home. This was the case in the parable of the lost sheep. (2) God does NOT pursue us (in our straying) when we are lost, but do KNOW the way home. This was the case in the parable of the lost son. The original Christian understanding of love and salvation (in the Eastern Church) is different in many ways, to what is presented in many protestant circles today. One problem from the offset is the idea of "forced love" (what some Calvinists call "irresistible grace"), which is not true love because love must be freely given.

> The early Church Fathers affirmed the role of free will in our salvation. One of the earliest pieces of Christian literature, the second century Letter to Diognetus, contains a clear affirmation of human free will and a rejection of salvation by compulsion. The author writes concerning the Incarnation: "He sent him as God; he sent him as man to men. He willed to save man by persuasion, not by compulsion, for compulsion is not God's way of working." [119]

Where there is no freedom, there can be no love. Compulsion excludes love; as Paul Evdokimov used to say, *God can do everything except compel us to love him.* [120]

LOVE MUST BE FREE INDEED TO BE LOVE IN TRUTH! This is also the assessment of Fr. James Bernstein in an excellent article on the subject, entitled: "The original Christian Gospel." [121] Not only is GOD LOVE, but God is humble! To say that God is humble is not an admission of Divine weakness. In fact, the very opposite is true. God's Almighty power is demonstrated in constraint; in Divine condescension for our sake and for our salvation. Coinciding with this common misunderstanding of love and freedom is another common misunderstanding: the cause of death. If we believe that death is somehow a curse from God (i.e. that God punished mankind with death because of sin), then we are tempted to believe that God Himself is the ultimate obstacle that we must overcome to gain salvation. The truth is this. Death came upon all men because of man's rejection of life (through disobedience to God's Word). Disobedience disconnected mankind from God who is the only source of life. Death is simply the natural result of willful disconnection (relationally) from the source of life. Another common misconception is that God needed to be appeased by the death of Jesus on the cross. That is not true! The cross was all about *atonement,* not *appeasement.* "God was IN CHRIST reconciling the world unto Himself" (2 Corinthians 5:19). Clearly, if God was not in Christ reconciling the world unto Himself, then the goal would become how to appease an angry God. God is love and humble and does not need to be appeased (as in the case of pagan deities). Renowned author and lecturer Metropolitan Kallistos (Timothy) Ware expressed it this way: *"It is natural for God to be humble as it is to be Almighty. God is as humble as He is Almighty."* The Scriptures speak of

God's humility in Philippians 2:5-8. We have already looked at this in some detail in the first half of this book:

> Let this mind be in you which was also in Christ Jesus, who, being in the form of God, did not consider it robbery [or something to be held onto] to be equal with God, but made Himself of no reputation [literally: "emptied Himself"], taking the form of a bondservant, and coming in the likeness of men. And being found in appearance as a man, He humbled Himself and became obedient to the point of death, even the death of the cross.

As previously stated, we strongly disagree with Edwards "God abhors you" characterization. If that were so – we might imagine that we needed to be saved from God more than from our sins. That would be ludicrous! We (as sinners) do NOT need to be saved FROM God, but are saved BY God. Fr. George Morelli put it this way, "we are not 'sinners in the hands of an angry God,' but rather sinners in the hands of a gentle and loving God!" [122] Jesus in His own words said,

> *Come to Me, all you who labor and are heavy laden, and I will give you rest. Take My yoke upon you and learn from Me, for I am gentle and humble [lowly] in heart, and you will find rest for your souls (Matthew 11:28, 29).*

> Jesus also said, *you have heard that it was said, you shall love your neighbor and hate your enemy. But I say to you, love your enemies... that you may be sons of your Father in heaven (Matthew 5:43–45).*

Jesus is telling us that we should love our enemies because God the Father loves His enemies. Even from the cross of the crucified God-Man, our Lord Jesus prayed for His enemies, saying, *"Forgive them, for they know not what they do!"* In loving our enemies, Jesus said that we become sons of our Father in heaven (i.e. we become godlike; truly children of God). The concluding verse says, *"for He (i.e. the Father) makes His sun rise on the evil and on the good."* St. Anthony the Great of Egypt (founder of monasticism in the fourth century), stated it perfectly: *"To say that God turns away from the wicked is like saying that the sun hides itself from the blind."* The all-pervasive love of God is and was the main theme of the original Gospel. How sad that it has become clouded and misunderstood – particularly over the last millennium (both within medieval Catholicism and Protestantism). There are many reasons for this – but perhaps one reason is core: The western church has often forgotten that "sin is… the failure to realize life as love and communion; the failure to be whole, healthy, complete.

> **Sin is the rejection of personal communion with God. Sin is restricting ourselves, isolating ourselves to live autonomous, independent, and self-sufficient lives. In a sense, sin is an obsessive 'self-love.' The absolute autonomy of the individual is sin, indeed the 'original sin.' Our offense against God is not that we have 'offended His honor,' but rather that we have turned from life itself. Sin is the denial of God's image in man and of God Himself. It is self-destructive. God hates sin, not because of what it does to Him, but because of what it does to us.** [123]

GOOD, GOOD FATHER:
(Shifting our understanding)

> **And he arose, and came to his father. But when he was yet a great way off, his father saw him, and had compassion, and ran, and fell on his neck, and kissed him (Luke 15:20).**

It is surprising to some to learn that the original Gospel—the Good News preached by Jesus Christ and His disciples—is different in some ways, from what is prominently presented in contemporary American Christianity. For many Christians, hearing this original Gospel will involve a major paradigm shift—a radical change in assumptions about God and about salvation. The original Christian Gospel begins with—love. We have been saying this from the very start of this book. John 3:16-17 says: *"For God so loved the world that He gave His only begotten Son, that whoever believes in Him should not perish but have everlasting life. For God, did not send His Son into the world to condemn the world, but that the world through Him might be saved."* The Benson Commentary makes the following remarks:

> <u>But when he was yet a great way off</u> — Having only come within sight of home, and his nakedness, and the consciousness of his folly, probably, making him ashamed to proceed further, his father — Happening to be looking that way; saw him — Before any of the rest of his family were aware of the circumstance; and had compassion (meaning: his bowels yearned) to observe the wretched condition he was in; and immediately, as if he had forgotten the dignity of his own character, and all the injuries he had received, he ran to his child, and fell on his neck and kissed him. The son advanced diffidently and slowly, under a burden of shame and fear; but the father ran to meet him with his encouragements. This shows our heavenly Father's desire of the conversion of sinners, and his readiness to meet them that are coming toward him. His eyes are on those that go astray from him, he is continually looking to see whether they will return to him, and marks and cherishes the first inclinations which they manifest so to do. [124]

Consider Barnes notes here:

> "<u>He arose, and came</u>" – Was coming. But here is no indication of "haste." He did not "run," but came driven by his wants, and, as we may suppose, filled with shame, and even with some doubts whether his father would receive him.
>
> "<u>A great way off</u>" – This is a beautiful description: the image of his father's happening to see him clad in rags, poor, and emaciated, and yet he recognized "his son," and all the feelings of a father prompted him to go and embrace him.
>
> "<u>Had compassion</u>" – Pitied him. Saw his condition: his poverty and his wretched appearance, and was moved with compassion and love.
>
> "<u>And ran</u>" – This is opposed to the way the son came. The beauty of the picture is greatly heightened by these circumstances. The son came slowly - the father "ran." The love and joy of the old man were so great that he hastened to meet him and welcome him to his home.
>
> "<u>Fell on his neck</u>" – Threw his arms around his neck and embraced him.
>
> "<u>And kissed him</u>" – This was a sign at once of affection and reconciliation, which must at once have dissipated every doubt of the son about the willingness of his father to forgive and receive him. A kiss is a sign of affection. [125]

Let us now turn our attention to the Elder Brother and contrast the loving, gracious attitude of the father with the condemning, moralizing, religious attitude of the Elder Brother (what we call the "Elder Brother Syndrome"). The Elder brother did not share his father's joy. In fact, he didn't even join the party. He was the perennial "good kid" who looked down his nose on everyone who got into trouble by making terrible choices. When his father came out to get call him into the feast, he refused by complaining... *"All these years I've slaved for you and never once refused to do a single thing you told me to. And in all that time you never gave me even one young goat for a feast with my friends. Yet when this son of yours comes back after squandering your money on prostitutes, you celebrate by killing the fattened calf!"*

COMBATING THE RELIGIOUS SPIRIT
(Performance v/s Belonging)

The older brother became angry and refused to go in. So his father went out and pleaded with him. But he answered his father, 'Look! All these years I've been slaving for you and never disobeyed your orders. Yet you never gave me even a young goat so I could celebrate with my friends (Luke 15:28-29).

The father heart of God stands in stark contrast to the heart of Pharisee-ism (the sect that hijacked Judaism in the time of

Christ; coming into existence a couple hundred years prior to the birth of Christ). Jesus' main battle was with the religious community (Scribes and Pharisees) of His day, not with the common, everyday sinners on the street. Jesus ate with publicans and sinners – but reserved His harshest rhetoric for the Pharisees. One example of just how far off the mark Pharisee-ism departed from true Judaism (i.e. the faith of Abraham), consider a few short phrases from a traditional Jewish prayer book:

> *Blessed are you, Hashem, King of the Universe, for not having made me a Gentile. Blessed are you, Hashem, King of the Universe, for not having made me a slave. Blessed are you, Hashem, King of the Universe, for not having made me a woman.* This "traditional" prayer was (and in some places still is) prayed every morning by Jews around the world. [127]

The Gospels show this tendency back in the time of Christ. The Bible makes it clear that Pharisees don't pray to God (in reality), but pray with themselves (self-centered prayers). The following text is proof of this statement. *"<u>The Pharisee stood by himself and prayed</u>: 'God, I thank you that I am not like other people – robbers, evildoers, adulterers, or even like this tax collector" (Luke 18:11).* Notice how Pharisee-ism identifies with their negation (i.e. what they were against) rather than their affirmation (i.e. what they were for). This is the root of self-righteousness and the root of sin. Such a condescending, negative contrast with others is indeed repugnant to God and best characterizes/explains God's love-wrath against such things. Paul said, *"we do not dare to classify or compare ourselves with some who commend themselves. When they measure themselves by themselves and compare themselves with themselves, they are not wise"* (2 Corinthians 10:12). In the parable of the prodigal son, the father clearly received not one, but two heartaches from the actions of his younger son: (a) the selfish act itself, but also (b) the underlying rejection that motivated such an unloving demand in the first place. We can so easily grieve God; the perfectly good and benevolent God who has loved us from eternity and given Himself for us in Christ His Beloved Son for our salvation on the cross. Only a loving God CAN BE grieved. Only a loving God CAN BE quenched. Think about that! God is so relational that He gives us the following commands. If He were impervious to such things, such a command would not exist. To God, everything is personal.

> *And do not <u>grieve</u> the Holy Spirit of God, by whom you were sealed for the day of redemption* (Eph. 4:30 ESV).

> *Do not <u>quench</u> the Holy Spirit* (1 Thessalonians 5:19).

> (Implied) *Do not <u>resist</u> the Holy Spirit* (Acts 7:51)

TALE OF TWO PRODIGALS
(Sinful prodigal; Religious prodigal)

In this story, we find (actually) the tale of two prodigals. The younger son was a prodigal in the tradition sense: given to sinful desires and pleasures. But what is often overlooked is the fact that the Elder Brother was also a prodigal too, but in a non-traditional sense. The Elder brother was caught in self-righteous hypocrisy and judgment of others. Jesus said: *"John came to you in the way of righteousness, and you did not believe him, but the tax collectors and the prostitutes believed him"* (v. 32a, from Matthew 21:28–32). As the parable ends, everything seems backwards. The sinner (the younger son) comes home to reconciliation and the "righteous," whereas the Elder Brother leaves home (apparently) never to return home again. You might way – in this story, the lost is found and the found is lost.

Everything is backwards. But the point is clear. God is a friend to sinners (who know they are sinners). This is amplified elsewhere in the Gospel narratives.

> Jesus went on to say, 'To what, then, can I compare the people of this generation? What are they like? They are like children sitting in the marketplace and calling out to each other: "We played the pipe for you, / and you did not dance; / we sang a dirge, / and you did not cry." For John, the Baptist came neither eating bread nor drinking wine, and you say, "He has a demon." The Son of Man came eating and drinking, and you say, "Here is a glutton and a drunkard, a friend of tax collectors and sinners" (Luke 7:31–34; cf. Matthew 11:16–19).

Another lesson we draw from the above passage is that no matter what Jesus did, Israel (God's chosen people) refused to respond to their Messiah and Savior. *"We played the pipe for you – but you did not dance." "We sang a dirge – and you did not cry."* Notice that willful response is necessary in God's dealings with man. We see this at work in both prodigals. We see two sons living at home; neither one knowing the heart of their father. Whatever the father did – they misunderstood, misinterpreted, misread. They didn't know their father! Is this not the sad condition of fallen mankind? In the case of the younger son, he did not "know" the love and grace of the father that surrounded him daily. He took the father for granted. Jesus said that "it rains upon the just and the unjust" (Matthew 5:45). In the case of the Elder Brother, he did not know the heart of the Father either. Consider these words: *"My son, the father said, you are always with me, and everything I have is yours" (Luke 15:31).* To summarize the problem:

1. The Younger Son had everything – but took it for granted and squandered it through licentious living. But because he came home – the lost was found.
2. The Elder Son had everything – but he walked away from fellowship because he refused to forgive. Therefore, the found was lost.

Something that is often overlooked here is the gracious attitude of the father towards both his sons. Noticed the similar action of the father towards both sons:

- Towards the younger son: *"But while he was still a long way off, his father saw him and was filled with compassion for him; he ran to his son, threw his arms around him and kissed him" (Luke 15:20).*

- Towards the Elder son: *"The older brother became angry and refused to go in. So, his father went out and pleaded with him" (Luke 15:28).*

Such is the goodness of our gracious God; what we call *common grace*. *"The LORD is good to all; he has compassion on all he has made" (Psalm 145:9).* God loves us and provides for us NOT because of us – but because that's just the way HE IS! I love words of the excellent worship chorus by Don Moen which says:

> Think about His love. Think about His goodness. Think about His Grace that's brought us through. For as high as the heavens above. So, great is the measure of our Father's love. Great is the measure of our Father's love. [128]

GOD IS GOOD and His mercy endures forever! This is the underlying theology of the Judeo-Christian tradition; which is the revelation of the "real" God.

GOD'S STEADFAST MERCY
(Covenant-love and loyalty)

> *... his father saw him and was filled with compassion for him; he ran to his son, threw his arms around him and kissed him (Luke 15:20).*

As we continue to consider this parable closely, we see how it ties into a consistent theme about God in Scripture; His mercy, goodness, compassion and love. In Luke 15:20, the Greek word for compassion is *splagxnízomai (*meaning literally: *"the inward parts, especially the nobler entrails; the heart, lungs, liver, and kidneys."* [129] In the four Gospels, it says that Jesus was "moved with compassion" and did something. Everything Jesus did was out of the motivation of compassion. We find here an important principle at work; one that originates in the Old Testament. Jesus was (and is) compassionate because God is merciful, loving and good. In the Old Testament, the word often translated "mercy" (in English) is based on the Hebrew word: *"chesed"* – translated into English as *"charity, favor, kindness (i.e. incomprehensible kindness), goodness, loving-kindness, steadfast affection, love, friendship, undeserved blessing, strong love, loyalty, faithful love, devotion."* Although this word *(chesed)* is not used in this parable (Luke 15), it is most certainly implied. The compassion of Christ in Luke 15:20 is directly related to God's *chesed* love. When we combine two words: love and grace, we arrive at this one word *chesed.* The word *chesed* is repeated some 223 times in the Old Testament (in the Psalms, about 100 times). The Greek equivalent of this word is *"charis"* (grace) and is used approximately 60 times in the New Testament. By some counts, the word "mercy" is used 283 times. All this to show that God is good. When Moses said to God (Exodus 33) *"show me your glory,"* God said in response: *"I will cause all my goodness to pass before you."* Then He said... *"I *will show mercy on whom I will show mercy."* There is a wonderful contemporary worship chorus by modern writer Chris Tomlin, entitled: "Good, Good Father" which beautifully describes this eternal truth: [130]

> Oh, I've heard a thousand stories of what they think you're like, but I've heard the tender whisper of love in the dead of night, and you tell me that you're pleased, and that I'm never alone
>
> You're a Good, Good Father, it's who you are, it's who you are, it's who you are, and I'm loved by you
> It's who I am, it's who I am, it's who I am
>
> Oh, and I've seen many searching for answers far and wide, but I know we're all searching for answers only you provide, cause you know just what we need
> Before we say a word
>
> Cause you are perfect in all of your ways
> You are perfect in all of your ways
> You are perfect in all of your ways to us

The character of God as revealed in Scripture stands in stark contrast to the gods (so-called) of other world religions (i.e. heathen gods). Here are a few examples:

> Buddhists believe that to reach Nirvana, a transcendental state of bliss, a person must follow the Noble Eightfold Path. This process of personal effort and discipline will end suffering for the individual.
>
> Hindus believe that one reaches Moksha—freedom from this world and the cycle of death and reincarnation—by

practicing self-sacrifice, meditation, and certain levels of self-realization.

Muslims believe that Allah grants Paradise to those who live a life of moral uprightness, using the Five Pillars as basic guidelines. [131]

Again, let us remember the compassion of the father. This was the heart of God on display. This narrative stands in contrast to what some consider a more normal harsh reaction in eastern culture under such circumstances. Eastern fathers would not normally act compassionately under these circumstances. The prodigal son should (they think) have been beaten or thrown out of the house. It was to be expected that he would be excommunicated. But such was not the case. The father (representing God) did not excommunicate the prodigal, but humbled himself and ran toward his son to embrace him. It was not God, but the prodigal who excommunicated himself. This has a powerful soteriological implication. It was the prodigal who sent himself into self-imposed exile away from the father's love. This leads to an important discussion about the state of mankind in the afterlife; both Believer and Unbeliever, heaven and hell.

CONCEPTIONS OF THE AFTERLIFE:
(The lens of C.S. Lewis)

One of the most enduring depictions of hell in the Western Church is borrowed from images that arise from such classic literature as *Dante's inferno;* which portrays hell as a place of material fire. It is clear, however, from Scripture, that hell is a spiritual place for the departed souls of the lost – and those who suffer there do so without God's delight. There is no legitimate fear-based evangelism. "The Lord is not slack concerning his promise, as some men count slackness; but is longsuffering to us-ward, not willing that any should perish, but that all should come to repentance." (2 Peter 3:9). Contrary to some modern evangelicals, the Gospel must not be presented in such a way as to fear-monger people into heaven by threatening hell. How different is that approach to that of our Lord Jesus, who wept over Jerusalem? *"O Jerusalem, Jerusalem, the city that kills the prophets and stones those who are sent to it! How often would I have gathered your children together as a hen gathers her brood under her wings, and you were not willing!" (Matthew 23:37).*

To show just how far afield the western church had gone by the time of the high middle ages, consider the ceiling of the Sistine Chapel (the large papal chapel built within the Vatican between 1477 and 1480 by Pope Sixtus IV). The ceiling's various painted elements form part of a larger decorated scheme which includes the large fresco known as "The Last Judgment" (see picture on next page) and is considered a cornerstone work of High Renaissance art on the sanctuary wall, as painted by Michelangelo. This is one of the things gone wrong with Western Christianity at the height of the Middle Ages. On this painting, it can be seen in cartoon form, a vision of human souls, not only suffering in extreme torture, but being prodded by red devils with tiny horns, cloven hoofs for feet, spiraling tails, and pitchforks at hand. The depictions are amazingly graphic and disturbing! Is this the way it really is for the damned in the next life? As we already stated, in our opinion, the answer is *no*. The problem with Latin/western church theology, especially in the high medieval period, was this flawed concept of an "angry God" who eternally punishes the wicked in an *active* way, as retribution for sin. Even the Protestant Reformers picked up on this theme (being "children" of the Roman Catholic Church). That characterization is inconsistent with God's love and finds its best correction in the Trinitarian theology of Orthodoxy.

132

It is fair to say that the Eastern Church has been the faithful and consistent communicator of God's essential nature being "love" down through church history. Certainly, there have been many Western Church scholars and writers who have faithfully presented God in the light of His love: including famed 20th century British writer and Oxford professor: C.S. Lewis (e.g. "The Great Divorce"), which is an important counterbalance to Dante's Infernal (from the Divine Comedy). [133] We also recommend the writings of modern day Anglican author, scholar; N.T. Wright. Lewis and Wright see hell as self-chosen destiny and the suffering of the interior consequences of rejecting God's life. In making only a few passing contrasts between Dante and Lewis: Dante's Inferno is a journey through Hell, whereas Lewis' Great Divorce is a journey through Heaven and Hell, although Lewis spends most of his time in heaven. Lewis, in regard to heaven, observed two important things:

First, in "The Great Divorce," George MacDonald tells the narrator, "Heaven is reality itself" (chapter 9, paragraph 27) whereas hell is "unreality." Second, the meaning of heaven, according to Lewis, is "blessed participation in that Life by a created spirit" (Mir, chapter 16, paragraph 25), (meaning: life is being in the presence of God). This gets to the heart of the matter regarding Lewis' description of the damned.

> Lewis images hell as a large, gray city, where it is always rainy and constantly in that stage of twilight just as the lights are being turned on. The narrator walks through empty streets lined with dingy boarding houses, small tobacco shops, windowless warehouses, and "bookshops of the sort that sell The Works of Aristotle" (chap. 1). The narrator joins a queue at a bus stop and boards a bus that takes him to the outskirts of heaven. We don't see hell again, but we learn more about it as the story continues. The citizens of the city are quarrelsome—fights break out, even on the bus, and we are told that the streets are empty as residents keep moving further away from each other because they can't stop quarreling with neighbors. We also learn that the city is unsubstantial.
> One can construct a house or come by various commodities just by thinking them, but the houses can't keep out rain or intruders and the commodities don't satisfy needs. Most striking is the fact that, though the gray city seems huge, it actually is tiny— "nearly nothing" (see chapter 9, paragraph 51). Lewis says (in chapter 13, paragraph 47) that "all Hell is smaller than one pebble of [the] earthly world." The focus of the book is not so much on imaging hell as on explaining why some souls are in hell, and why they choose to return there even when they are offered the opportunity to stay in heaven. The souls are not condemned to hell as punishment: they put themselves into hell. As the

character, George MacDonald tells the narrator, "All that are in Hell, choose it. Without that self-choice, there could be no Hell. No soul that seriously and constantly desires joy will ever miss it" (chapter 9, paragraph 41). The book concentrates on two characteristic hellish attitudes. One is self-centeredness. Damned souls are totally wrapped up in themselves, and as they turn increasingly inward, they grow smaller and smaller. "A damned soul is nearly nothing," MacDonald notes. "It is shrunk, shut up in itself." The other is un-love. Hell, is characterized by degraded forms of love—jealousy, possessiveness, manipulative-ness. Instead of reaching out to others in love, damned souls love only themselves and as they become more and more self-absorbed, they become smaller and smaller.

The images are consistent with the ideas another C.S. Lewis book entitled: "The Problem of Pain." The essence of hell, according to Lewis, is not physical torture. The cynical ghost in "The Great Divorce" finds that disappointing: "They lead you to expect red fire and devils and all sorts of interesting people sizzling on grids… (he says), but when you get there it's just like any other town" (chapter 7, paragraph 14). The pain of hell is internal, the agony of literal self-absorption (growing ever less and less in personhood) and of resulting increases in quarrelsomeness and isolation. As souls become fixed in these attitudes, they are in hell. [134]

This is a good place to pick up our story on the Prodigal Son. Back-tracking just a bit: remember the prodigal son in the far country? *Hell,* is NOT ONLY a place unbelievers go upon death, but hell is a progressively disintegrating condition that begins in this present life which continues into the next life. Hell, is characterized by increasing self-centeredness, isolation and meaningless. To be in isolation (without meaningful relationship with others) is a sure way to lose one's personhood. This gets to the heart of the problem for the prodigal son. He was in isolation in the far country before he came home. What was happening there? The lost son was slowly but surely being de-personalized, de-humanized. He was in "hell" (in a metaphoric sense). This leads us to consider a more basic question then: how do we define personhood?

DEFINING PERSONHOOD
(A being in relationship)

What does it mean to be a "person"? The true definition of a person is a "being in relationship," dynamic, interactive, loving and serving. Personhood is the sense of self (the ego) in relation to another (the non-ego). This is personhood. This is also true of the triune God in whose image we are made.

> Christian systematician Louis Berkhof, quoting William G. T. Shedd, argues for the general self-consciousness of the triune God, as distinguished from the particular individual self-consciousness of each one of the Persons in the Godhead. For in self-consciousness, the subject must know itself as an object, and also perceive that it does. This is possible in God because of His trinal (tri-personal) existence. God could not be self-contemplating, self-cognitive, and self-communing, if He were not trinal in His constitution." [135] Shedd explains that among men, the *ego* awakens to consciousness only by contact with the *non-ego* (i.e. another person who is not myself). Personality does not develop nor exist in isolation, but only in association with other persons. Hence, it is not possible to conceive of personality in God apart from an association of equal persons in Him. Paul speaks of the

pleroma (fullness) of the Godhead in Ephesians 3:19 and Colossians 1:9, 2:9. In view of the fact that there are three persons in God, it is better to say that God is personal than to speak of Him as a person. [136]

As we consider the sad state of the prodigal son as he flees into a far country – we see immediately that he was in a disintegrating, de-humanizing and de-personalizing state of affairs – a slow motion death. Death is the privation of life just as isolation is the privation of relationship. We were created for inter-personal relationship and fellowship. God (who is personal) waits (like the father in the parable) at the end of the driveway – anticipating the reconciliation and the renewal of fellowship. When the prodigal son's vague and bedraggled silhouette became visible against the evening skyline, the father did something unusual for ancient elders; he girded up his loins and ran towards his son to greet him. This is what we call *"the scandal of God's grace."* To explain this, we must remember the honor/shaming culture of the ancient world.

The culture of middle-eastern communities in that day (as it remains today) was one of honor and shame. Honor was connected to how one was perceived in the community. The prodigal son had brought shame on his father and his whole family by his behavior, and thus could be expected to be shamed by the entire village as well. In the tradition of that day, the towns people would gather around such a returning prodigal and conduct a *"Gesasah Ceremony,"* which was anything but a welcome home ceremony. Rather, it was a "shaming-ceremony" that involved "breaking jars with corn and nuts and declare that he was to be cut off from the village. His entry into the village would be humiliating as his townspeople expressed their anger and resentment toward his actions." He was to them one as good as dead! [137] In some instances, families would go to the extent of committing a "mercy-killing" in that culture. The life of the returning prodigal was threatened at the hands of villagers were it not for the compassion of the awaiting father at the end of the road; not only to restore, but to rescue him from such a certain ordeal. The father put his very life and reputation on the line, yet again. The first time – when the boy first committed the selfish act. And now a second time in protecting the son upon his return. It was *the scandal of grace* that exposed not only the returning prodigal, but the gracious father to ridicule. It reminds us of Mount Calvary and the shame that Jesus bore on our behalf for our salvation. This is the love of God in action for His beloved.

> He was despised and rejected by mankind, a man of suffering, and familiar with pain. Like one from whom people hide their faces he was despised, and we held him in low esteem. Surely he took up our pain and bore our suffering, yet we considered him punished by God, stricken by him, and afflicted. But he was pierced for our transgressions, he was crushed for our iniquities; the punishment that brought us peace was on him, and by his wounds we are healed. We all, like sheep, have gone astray, each of us has turned to our own way; and the Lord has laid on him the iniquity of us all. (Isa. 53:3-6).

THE RUNNING FATHER:
(Pursuing love of God)

But while he was still a long way off, his father saw him and... he ran to his son... (Luke 15:20).

In modern western culture, children routinely leave homes in the country to pursue their future and their fortune in big cities, or even abroad. But as we have just explained, in the time of Christ, this kind of action in the culture of the middle east, would have been considered extremely shameful; with the younger son abandoning his obligation to care for his father in his old age. There were norms that were not to be violated. And yet, this reminds us of exactly what Israel did in apostatizing against the covenant of God (initiated in Abraham and solidified in Moses). It was unthinkable for them to do this before God! How could the ONLY chosen people in the earth have made such a choice to reject the God of love and grace? But they did – and so did all humanity. "There is no one righteous, not even one" (Romans 3:10). Earlier in the story we know that the son had fled into a foreign country, wasted his money and found himself in trouble as his degradation reached new low point: he ate with pigs. Please understand, for a Jew to have anything to do with un-kosher pigs was bad enough, but for a Jewish boy to feed pigs and seek to eat pig-food out of desperation, was beyond imaginable. And yet, for all this, the most remarkable person in the story is not the prodigal son, but the gracious favor of the father. This is really the parable of "the running father."

In a culture where senior citizens were far too dignified to run anywhere, this elder man in the story takes to his heels as soon as he sees his young son dragging himself home. It was unthinkable (in the normal custom of their day) for an older man to gather up his robes (to gird up his loins – to use the words of the King James Version) and run towards his shameful son. The lavish welcome/reception (as opposed to a shaming ceremony) for the wayward son is the whole point of the story. Jesus is explaining why there must be a party – why there this was worth a celebration. The prodigal's degradation was complete (he went into a far country and spent all he had). There can be no question of anything in him commending him to his father, or to any other onlookers. He was utterly lost, undone, without hope in this world, worthy of shaming at least, and death at worth – all except for the unconditional love and unmerited favor of his father (which he had utterly forgotten, and certainly did not expect upon his return trip home). He probably hoped to merely survive the shaming ordeal and simply wind up with a seasonal job living off campus from the family ranch. In this, let us depart from the traditional evangelical interpretation of the returning prodigal and consider the real motivation of the prodigal in returning home. While it is okay to teach repentance at this point in the story (as traditionally presented), we want to present a different picture. Again, this parable can be taught as a beautiful picture of repentance; if seen from one angle. But in fact, the returning prodigal was not interesting in restored son-ship. We should not think that when he "came to himself" and returned home, it was because he was a sincere penitent. That would read too much into the story. The truth of the matter is that the boy was homeless and desperate. The wages of sin had driven him homeward to find seasonal work in order not to starve to death. If he still had money and/or gainful employment, he would have no doubt remained in the far country.

How often do we pray to God only as a last resort? This is the point here. The lost son had an entirely different internal dialogue than the father had in his mind. The boy returned home not with the motivation of being reconciled with his father – but to have seasonal work and live off campus so he could survive another season. The Prodigal Son was the original "survivor" in his own "reality show." For him, it was pure survival; economics. It was not about repentance. It was desperation. Regardless of the boy's pathetic speech, the father rejoiced just to get his boy into his arms. In the end, the father threw a party regardless of the motivation of the returning prodigal. Perhaps it's not so much about the initial motivation, but "whatever it takes" (regardless of motivation) to get us into the loving arms of God. I've seen people come to church and come to Christ under the strangest of circumstances. God is bigger than our preconceived ideas of Him. God can use anything and anyone to further His purposes. It's more about "turning around" and coming home under any condition. The therapy and twelve-step programs and such will all come later. The counseling and inner healing will come later. For now, just to be in the arms of the father, is what is important! None of us found Christ under perfect circumstances?

THE BEMA SEAT
(Rewards won or lost):

I hope this is not stretching the metaphor, but I can imagine the return of the prodigal to be something like the final judgment when/where we meet God face to face. While some people feel that the final judgment is at the time of death, orthodoxy teaches that the final judgment is at the Second Coming of Christ; which is at the end of the age, when Jesus returns to make all things new. I think there is an analogy between the prodigal coming home to the father and the final judgment: better interpreted – the *Bema Seat*. When we stand before God on that final day, I don't image there to be a super-sized movie screen rolling, where all our sins, mistake and failures are displayed for all to see. God is not in the shaming-business. I do not believe that the Bema Seat will be a cosmic *Gesasah-Ceremony*. Why? Because sin and shame has already been punished/vanquished at Calvary through the work of the cross. Our loving, gracious God in Christ has already suffered such an ordeal on our behalf. The issue at the Bema Seat, therefore, will not be if God will love us/embrace us, but will we allow the Father to embrace us? Will we return the hug? To put it another way, will we receive the unmerited grace of God to cover our rags and receive the garment of salvation through the finished work of Calvary? The Father is even now pursuing us (every one of us) as we slowly make our way back home. What will we do when we finally arrive at our heavenly home? Will we return the Divine embrace of grace or rely on our own self-righteousness and reject the gift of God? This is the cosmic question. This is what is ultimately at stake and symbolized here. For his part, the prodigal son returned the hug and received the grace of God and thus entered into eternal life. This Elder Brother, on the other hand, did not return the hug; did not forgive his brother, did not enter into the gracious party and chose rather to continue in his un-forgiveness and self-righteousness – and instigated a *shaming ceremony* on his brother in which the father refused to participate. The 'bema seat' (the judgment seat) for the Elder Brother, therefore, was the loss of all rewards. He did not walk in love. All his works/rewards were burned up in the fire. We should explain this truth and analogy more thoroughly. We must all make our appearance before our Creator eventually, regardless of our motivations. *"It is appointed unto men once to die, but after this the judgment" (Hebrews 9:27).* Again, the return of the prodigal can, I think, be likened also to the Bema Seat. *"We will all appear before the Judgment Seat" (Romans 14:10).* When we say "judgment," that word normally has ominous overtones to our western ears. But consider the reality in the light of Scripture.

> The expression "the judgment seat of Christ" in the English Bible has tended to cause some to draw the wrong conclusion about the nature and purpose of this evaluation. A common misconception which arises from this English translation is that God will mete out a just retribution for sins in the believer's life, and some measure of retributive punishment for sins will result. Though it is tremendously serious with eternal ramifications, the judgment seat of Christ is not a place and time when the Lord will mete out punishment for sins committed by the child of God. Rather, it is a place where rewards will be given or lost depending on how one has used his or her life for the Lord. [138]

The word judgment seat is from the Greek: *'bema'* which means 'a raised platform' reached by steps. In the ancient world, it was a speaker's platform. Therefore, churches usually have raised platforms where orations are given. Actually, a pulpit is a 'bema' where we come under the hearing of the preaching of God's Word. But something further is important here. In the New Testament, it seems that Paul was referring to something specific when speaking of the judgment seat of Christ. In classical Greek, the bema was the judge's seat in the arena of the Olympic games. It was NOT trial court or something like that. Rather, the 'bema' was the seat whereon the judge sat; not to punish contestants, but to present awards to the victors. Here is the spiritual connection. We are victorious, not because of our own conquest over sin and death, but through Christ's conquest over sin and death *for us* and *as us*. *"But thanks, be to God! He gives us the victory through our Lord Jesus Christ"* (1 Corinthians 15:57 NIV). *"We are more than conquerors through Him that loved us so"* (Romans 8:37). When we stand before the 'bema' of Christ, it will NOT be for inflicting punishment! It is not a shaming-ceremony! Rather, it will be for the express purpose of being rewarded according to our works; whether good or bad (which are either rewarded or not). So, then the next question obviously is – what then is our work which is worthy of reward? Jesus answered that question when He said: *"The work of God is this: to believe in the one he has sent" (John 6:29 NIV).* Faith is our work (i.e. "to believe") and love is its own reward.

> Love seeks one thing only: the good of the one loved. It leaves all the other secondary effects to take care of themselves. Love, therefore, is its own reward. – *Thomas Merton*

The Apostle Paul said that *"faith works by love" (Galatians 5:6).* In other words, true faith finds its deepest motivation and ultimate manifestation by and through love. Love is always an action verb. Love acts. Love works in deed and truth (1 John 3:18). Love requires obedience (John 14:15). Anything that is not motivated by love is worthless, according to the scriptures. *"If I speak in the tongues of men or of angels, but do not have love, I am only a resounding gong or a clanging cymbal. If I have the gift of prophecy and can fathom all mysteries and all knowledge, and if I have a faith that can move mountains, but do not have love, I am nothing. If I give all I possess to the poor and give over my body to hardship that I may boast, but do not have love, I gain nothing" (1 Corinthians 13:1-3 NIV).* Love is the measure of all worthy-things! Self-centeredness is the measure of all worthless things! This is the great revelation of life and eternal life. If we receive the grace of God and walk in the love of God, that is the law of new creation/the law of the Spirit of life in Christ Jesus. How we are rewarded, therefore, is measured by how we walk in the grace and love of God towards others in this life. Anything else is burned-up and worthless. In any event, there is no idea of punishment inflicted at the Bema Seat, but rather whether our works (faith, hope and love – these three remain – 1 Corinthians 13:13) will endure the ultimate test of fire (i.e. the purifying fires of Divine love) which is the universal standard because love is the essential nature of the triune God.

> For no one can lay any foundation other than the one already laid, which is Jesus Christ. If anyone builds on this foundation using gold, silver, costly stones, wood, hay or straw, their work will be shown for what it is, because the Day will bring it to light. It will be revealed with fire, and the fire will test the quality of each person's work. If what has been built survives, the builder will receive a reward. If it is burned up, the builder will suffer loss but will be saved--even though only as one escaping through the flames. (1 Cor. 3:11-15 NIV).

To summarize our earlier statements, The Bema Judgement is not for punishment based on sin, but rather an assessment of our servanthood (i.e. how well we have executed our responsibility as heirs to the Kingdom to walk in faith and love. Consider what we know here per the Scripture:

1. Subjects: Believers as to their works
2. Time: at Christ's Second Coming (1 Thess. 4:13-18)
3. Place: in heaven (1 Thessalonians 4:17)
4. Basis: our works (whether good or bad) (Revelation 19:8)
5. Result: rewards (gained or lost) (1 Corinthians 3:11 – 13)

It would require another study guide to expound on this important subject in greater detail. The bottom line is that Christ has already taken our punishment at Calvary. We should purge our thoughts of a "punishing God" mentality. Paul asks: "who then can condemn us" (Romans 8:34)? Paul is not suggesting that Jesus Christ condemns us. Quite the opposite. Paul is saying that Jesus Christ is the only one who could possibly condemn us, except for the fact that He took our judgment upon Himself. That's what love does and that's what love did! To receive the knowledge of that truth is what makes us free and free indeed! This is the glorious news of Romans 8:1. To receive it is life and peace. To deny it is to exile ourselves much like the prodigal son did in the beginning of the story. Notice that the prodigal had created an "idol" in his mind; an idol-father of rejection and retribution. But that was a lie.

The true father is not like that. When sinners come home, however they ultimately come home, they come home to a waiting father, a running father, a father with arms outstretched, a grace which needs only be believed and received. This is the Divine posture. The father didn't roll up his sleeves into a fist. He was <u>not</u> distempered, punitive or calculating. He was not preparing for, or participating in a *shaming-ceremony*.

Rather, the father was already in a swift sprint with arms outreached; closing the gap between the wayward son and Himself. This is the true nature of God, the true heart of God and the Good News of the Gospel. God has closed the gap between sinners and Himself through the cross. This is redemption's story and the heart of God.

THE GLORIOUS GOSPEL:
(The Good News)

Once again, we encounter the heart of the GOSPEL (Gr. *euaggelion,* from which we get our word "evangelistism." *Euaggelion* means "good news, glad tidings." William Tyndale, the 16th century English scholar martyred at the age of 42 for translating the Bible into English, defined the Gospel this way:

> That good, merry, glad and joyful tidings, that maketh a man's heart glad, and maketh him sing, dance and leap for joy. [139]

How's that for a Gospel definition/declaration from the mouth of a true Christian saint and martyr? No one is truly prepared to *die* for the Gospel who is not first prepared to *live* for the Gospel. The Gospel is the announcement of some prior action done. The Gospel is NOT about something we must do to gain God's acceptance and love. THE GOSPEL IS WHAT GOD SAYS ABOUT THE SITUATION, not what we say about it!

- Here is the situation according to the prodigal: *"The son said to him, 'Father, I have sinned against heaven and against you. I am no longer worthy to be called your son"* *(Luke 15:21).*

- Here is the situation according to the father: *"the father said to his servants, 'Quick! Bring the best robe and put it on him. Put a ring on his finger and sandals on his feet. Bring the fattened calf and kill it. Let's have a feast and celebrate. For this son of mine was dead and is alive again; he was lost and is found" (Luke 15:22-24).*

The Gospel is something we hear, believe and receive. It's already done! It is finished! The Gospel is based on what God in Christ has already done for us! Our actions (or reactions) don't change anything. Ours is to accept and receive the father's embrace. This is the good news! This is the Gospel! Our sins are all taken away. St. Paul said, *"I delivered unto you that which I received: that Christ died for our sins according to the Scriptures" (1 Corinthians 15:3).*

IT IS FINISHED!
(Sin has been conquered)

"There is a truly glorious word in Greek that speaks of the completeness of Christ's work on the Cross: Tetelestai: It is finished! Literally translated the word *tetelestai* means, "It is finished." The word occurs in John 19:28 and 19:30 and these are the only two places in the New Testament where it occurs. In 19:28 it is translated, "After this, when Jesus knew that all things were now completed, in order that the scripture might be fulfilled, he said, 'I thirst.'" Two verses later, he utters the word himself: "Then when he received the sour wine Jesus said, 'It is finished,' and he bowed his head and gave up his spirit." The word *tetelestai* was also written on business documents or receipts in New Testament times to show indicating that a bill had been paid in full. The Greek-English lexicon by Moulton and Milligan says this:

Receipts are often introduced by the phrase [sic] tetelestai, usually written in an abbreviated manner... (p. 630). The connection between receipts and what Christ accomplished would have been quite clear to John's Greek-speaking readership; it would be unmistakable that Jesus Christ had died to pay for their sins. [140]

In Bible times, when someone paid off his bill in the marketplace, he would run through the streets shouting *"tetelestai, tetelestai, my debt is paid in full!"* When Jesus was on the cross, His last words were, *"It is finished," (tetelstai);* the debt is paid-in-full. Jesus was referring to the debt for our sins. Jesus paid the debt for our sins in full on the cross – totally and completely, always and for all time!" [141] Now that's the Gospel! That's the Good News! We are NOT preaching the Gospel when we tell people what they must do to find favor with God! We are NOT preaching the Gospel when we tell people what they must commit to stop doing to find forgiveness with God. We have it backwards when we do so. Consider the following two concepts in contrast. The first one is incorrect. The second one is correct. Many evangelicals fail to fully comprehend this truth.

- LEGAL REPENTANCE (the incorrect way) says that "if" we repent, then and only then will God forgive us. This "if-then" approach is based upon the false notion that our action, our repentance, somehow conditions God's heart to forgive us. This is a works-righteousness approach which takes the action away from God and Calvary and places it on us. This approach incorrectly assumes that God is unforgiving towards us "until" we repent and make satisfaction for our sins, rather than realizing that God in Christ has already made satisfaction in our stead "in Christ" on Calvary.

- **EVANGELICAL REPENTANCE (the correct way)** puts the emphasis where it belongs – away from us and upon Christ. Evangelical repentance (gospel repentance) says: because God has already forgiven you in Christ, therefore, repent and believe/receive the Gospel. This "because-therefore" approach starts with the "finished work of Christ" and proclaims the Good News from that standpoint. With the Gospel of grace understood, the proclamation becomes: repent and RECEIVE your pardon/forgiveness which is already yours in Christ, although we must personally receive it to benefit from it. Forgiveness is the response of faith, not its product. Forgiveness is only and always the product of grace. [142]

As the prodigal returned home – notice that the father did not immediately confront his son about his sin before the embrace. That would come later. The "therapy" would come later. For now, what the boy needed was unconditional love. The prodigal was already forgiven by the father before the boy even understood how to repent properly – even before the boy had the right motivation for returning home in the first place. The Good News is that God has forgiven us in Christ before (and in spite of) our understanding or even acceptance of it. Did the prodigal need repentance? Yes! Absolutely! Must we repent? But true repentance is not merely a single moment in time. Repentance is usually a growing process of (Gr. *metanoia*) "changing our mind about the truth." Repentance is a process and work of the Holy Spirit as we come around to the truth about the way things really are. Truth is reality. Repentance includes guilt and remorse, but does not stop there. This is yet another area where many evangelicals tend to get it wrong. We make repentance only as an emotional response rather than a thoughtful understanding and agreement with the truth. When we fully agree with the truth, our behavior will likewise change. Absolutely! A real acknowledgment of the truth will always produce a corresponding change of lifestyle, whether it happens quickly or gradually. We are not soft on sin or confession, rather we are emphasizing the true nature of repentance – which is to have a radical change of mind about the truth.

AVOIDING EXTREMES:
(Caution on either side)

At this point, I feel the need to give a strong word of caution. There is a "new" [143] heresy afoot especially popular in some charismatic circles today – otherwise known as the "hyper-grace" movement. It's funny when we say "new" because a generation ago, Dietrich Bonhoeffer; the great German pastor and theologian, was asked in 1943, how it was possible for the church to sit back and let Hitler and the Nazis seize absolute power. Bonhoeffer's reply: "It was the teaching of cheap grace." I think we have a similar manifestation today. From what I can tell (having not studied it as thoroughly as I plan to), there is a mixture of truth and error in the *hyper-grace* movement. Some of its purveyors are indeed quite popular today. To throw another word out there, it appears to be just a weaker, albeit contemporary version of "antinomianism." [144] If that characterization is correct; it perverts the true grace of God into a license for immorality at some point, regardless of how subtle. Christians beware! Holiness matters! Basically, antinomianism is an exaggeration of "justification by faith alone" by saying that obedience to God's law is unimportant. That is heresy! Too live under true grace is to be empowered to live ABOVE sin, not to be given a license to sin! Confession and repentance matters! The Lord's Prayer (the "our Father") is a legitimate and necessary prayer for today! I personally pray the Lord's Prayer every day. The Holy Spirit convicts and convinces of sin. The four Gospels matter, and not just the Pauline epistles. The Old Testament matters, and not just the New Testament. We believe the Psalms are the hymnbook and confessional of the church. We believe in heaven and hell, good and evil, righteousness and unrighteousness. Despite heresy (heresy is truth taken to an extreme), we must understand and rejoice in the finality of the cross and its death blow against sin. Daniel said, *"Seventy 'sevens are decreed for your people and your holy city to finish transgression, to put an end to sin, to atone for wickedness, to bring in everlasting righteousness, to seal up vision and prophecy and to anoint the Most Holy Place"* (Daniel 9:24). We must be careful not to venture into dangerous extremes on either side of this truth. Heresy is lurking both to the right and the left side of the Gospel of grace.

Here are the two equally dangerous extremes:

1. ANTINOMIANISM: Heresy on the right side: (hyper-grace), which says that the law doesn't matter and we can do what we want with no consequences. In this instance, grace gives us a license to sin. This was the Corinthian problem that Paul dealt with. This is contrasted with...

2. LEGALISM: Heresy on the left side: (Pharisee-ism), which says that the law saves us; i.e. that adherence to a strict set of religious rules saves us. This was the Galatian problem that Paul also had to deal with. Both extremes are wrong and a mutation of the true Gospel of our Lord Jesus Christ.

So, there we have it: the two extremes of the true Gospel of grace. Both will lead us down the path to destruction. We must not allow a *hyper-grace* message (an antinomian spirit) to drive us back into legalism and derail the true grace of God, and yet we must also avoid the *spirit of legalism* (i.e. Pharisee-ism, the Elder Brother syndrome). What is the balanced Gospel? It is the announcement that our sins are forgiven for His name sake, but that does not mean we can sin with impunity or don't need to confess our sins anymore! A thousand times – no! Rather, it means that God has already forgiven us in Christ and that when we do confess our sins (and we must confess our sins: 1 John 1:9), we are agreeing with God on the issue that it is finished! The primary Greek word for CONFESS *(homologeo)* basically means "to say the same thing" and then "agree, admit, acknowledge." [145] Psalm 103 says *"He's taken our sins and He's separated them from us as far as the east is from the west"* (Psalm 103:12). How far is that? Too far to calculate! We don't know how far the east is from the west, but however far that is, that's how far God has separated our sins from us. That's the Good News! Romans 8:1 says that *"There is therefore now no condemnation to them who are in Christ Jesus."*

John 5:24: *"Verily, verily, I say unto you, he that heareth My words and believeth on Him that sent Me hath everlasting life, and shall not come into condemnation, but is passed from death unto life."* The judgment for Believers is already past – already over. It fell on Jesus at the cross (1 Peter 2:24). God in Christ died in our stead (2 Corinthians 5:21). That's the Good News! The prodigal son did NOT know the Gospel. Rather, the prodigal son had created a false gospel (another gospel) in his head. The prodigal said to himself (and repeated it later to his father): *"I am no longer worthy to be called your son."* To make such a statement could mean in a legal and a moral sense that he felt he had no further rights for family acceptance. His behavior had not measured up to the family standards and thus (he assumed) his relationship with his father was based solely on his demerits. He had a legalistic than a relational mentality. He said, *"make me like one of your hired servants"* (i.e. he was willing to earn his keep by serving the family – which would mean serving his older brother, too. "Hired men" (hired servants: *misthioi,* are contract laborers – probably "farmhands" and not *douloi,* which are "household bondservants" mentioned in Luke 15:22. But the father's closing line in the story says it all. *'This my son was dead and is alive; he was lost and now is found.'* In the mind of the father (which is the attitude of our heavenly Father towards all His children, especially those who were lost, but are now found): HOW CAN THIS NOT BE A CAUSE FOR REJOICING?

WELCOME HOME:
(Returning from self-imposed exile)

One of the great stories of Israel's past, as previously stated, was the original Exodus; when Israel was brought out of Egypt and brought "home" (if you will) to the Promised Land. Now, many years later (centuries later), after a long rebellion, God's people Israel were sent into exile under Nebuchadnezzar in Babylon. And though many Israelites (the remnant) returned to their homeland, most of Jesus' contemporaries considered that they were indeed still in exile under Roman oppression (i.e. the gentiles were still ruling over them). This was what their Messianic fervor was all about; to be delivered from gentile oppression. The original audience that Jesus spoke to (the Jewish people) were awaiting a Messianic figure who would liberate them (after 500-years) from the political exile of their gentile overloads and restore their national sovereignty once and for all. This was the primary concern of the Jewish people and focus of their Messianic hope. Therefore, for Jesus to tell them a story about a prodigal son who was lost in a foreign land – who was welcomed back with a lavish party – was certainly, understood to reference the perennial "hope of Israel," which was their return from exile. The "hope of Israel" is a constant theme throughout both the Old and New Testaments. *This my son was dead, and is alive'* surely had the overtones of Ezekiel 37 and the idea of resurrection (the resurrection of old dead, dried out bones). This was picture-language for the true exilic return.

Some might even see it in Jesus' 'Born-Again' statements in John chapter three. Salvation is all about "life from the dead." But there was something infinitely greater than just nationalistic salvation in Jesus' message. What Jesus was driving at was eternal salvation from Satan and sin! The coming of Jesus Christ (God's Son our only Savior) into the world was not only salvation for the Jews, but salvation for the whole world. When people positively respond to the Good News, the true "return from the exile" occurs. In the coming of Jesus as the Messiah represented such a deliverance from exile (and it did), why not celebrate and be merry (as the parable commands). This was the imperative of the father. It was the only proper thing to do! But those to whom the Gospel was originally sent would have none of it! They missed their day of visitation, except for the remnant. This is another way of understanding this parable.

GRACIOUS GIFTS OF GOD:
(The unworthy made worthy)

As we now come to the close of our studies, let us concentrate on the gracious gifts of God and notice that God endows us with His very own righteousness, authority and pathway. *"... Bring forth the best robe, and put it on him; and put a ring on his hand, and shoes on his feet: and bring hither the fatted calf, and kill it..." (Luke 15:22-23).*

> God's giving always follows His forgiving. It is not so with us. We think ourselves very magnanimous when we pardon; and we seldom go on to lavish favors where we have overlooked faults. Perhaps it is right that men who have offended against men should earn restoration by acts, and should have to ride quarantine, as it were, for a time. But I question whether forgiveness is ever true which is not, like God's, attended by large-hearted gifts.

If pardon is only the non-infliction of penalty, then it is natural enough that it should be considered sufficient by itself, and that the evildoer should not be rewarded for having been bad. But if pardon is the outflow of the love of the offended to the offender, then it can scarcely be content with simply giving the debtor his discharge, and turning him into the world penniless. However, that may be with regard to men, God's forgiveness is essentially the communication of God's love to us sinners, as if we had never sinned at all. And, that being so, that love cannot stay its working until it has given all that it can bestow or we can receive. God does not do things by halves; and He always gives when He forgives. Now that is the great truth of the last part of this immortal parable. And it is one of the points in which it differs from, and towers high above, the two preceding ones. The lost sheep was carried back to the pastures, turned loose there, needed no further special care, and began to nibble as if nothing had happened. The lost drachma (coin) was simply put back in the woman's purse. But the lost son was pardoned, and, being pardoned, was capable of receiving, and received, greater gifts than he had before. These gifts are remarkably detailed in the text.[146]

I.   First gift – THE ROBE: Restored Righteousness (right-relationship): *"... bring forth the best robe..."*

In the Scriptures, we find from beginning to end, a series of instances which lead us at once to understand the true meaning of "bring forth the best robe." In Zechariah, the prophet saw in vision the high priest standing at the heavenly tribunal, clothed in filthy garments and a voice said, *"Take away the filthy garments from him,"* and the interpretation is added: *"Behold! I have caused thine iniquity to pass from thee, and I will clothe thee with a change of raiment."* We should also remember the parable of Christ regards the wedding garment. We might also remember Paul's frequent metaphor about *"putting off the old man, putting on the new man."* We might also remember the visions of John the Revelator on the isle of Patmos, who saw the armies in heaven that followed Christ our victorious Commander in Chief: *"clothed in fine linen, white and pure, which is the righteousness of the saints."* All in all, the interpretation is clear. To come home to the father and accept our acceptance (which is not based on our own works, but on His grace, alone: the vicarious work of Christ at Calvary), is the basis for our righteousness. This is what the "robe" speaks of. It is the garment of salvation; the robe of righteousness.

    II.   Second gift – THE RING: Restored Authority (right actions): *"… put a ring on his hand…"*

The prodigal son had originally returned home (as we have already mentioned) intending merely to be placed in the position of a slave. But the father said, "put a ring on his finger." The ring is an emblem of wealth, position and honor. It is a sign of delegated authority. Authority is defined as "acting with proper permission." In other words, authority must not be confused with "raw power." It is not. Authority is power with permission. Authority is power under control. It is power with character. The signet ring is a sign of one who has received the honor and dignity of the one who gifted the ring to him (honor by association). A prime example of this is when Joseph was exalted to be the second man in Egypt, and Pharaoh's signet ring was taken from off his hand and placed upon Joseph's finger. Joseph received the honor of the king. Freedom, exaltation and dignity is restored in this way. A ring also has ornamental value – meaning that when God grants us pardon, He also restores our beauty in Christ. The overall meaning of the ring is that of restored authority and beauty in Christ.

III. Third gift – THE SANDALS: Restored walk (right direction): *"... and shoes on his feet..."*

No doubt the prodigal son had come back barefooted, filthy and bleeding. The path of the transgressor is hard, the Scriptures says. There are many trials and sorrows that we have experienced in our lives – some (many) self-inflicted. But the Good News of the Gospel comes along and gives us new sandals for our feet. The Gospel is this – our heavenly father is standing at the end of the driveway wanting to put new shoes on our feet (which represent the Gospel of peace) to wear to make straight our path. A very important part of the equipment of an ancient soldier was heavy boots, which enabled him to stand fast in the day of battle and resist the enemy's onslaught. This is what the father has clothed us with. *"That we may be able to withstand in the evil day, and having done all, to stand." (Ephesians chapter six).* The sandals speak of a restored walk (path) and the protection and guidance it brings along the road in the face of the trials of life.

MAKING IT PRACTICAL:
(Why God's love is primary)

The so called "Parable of the Prodigal Son" should be named the "Parable of the Compassionate Father and His Two Lost Sons." In many ways, this parable illustrates the relationship of every type of person to his or her Father in heaven. All mankind is thus featured in this great parable. All mankind is seen in the two sons. We are either the younger, or the elder, or a combination of both. The younger son is like so many people who do not want to be near religious faith. They choose their own way in rebellion. They run away from God and his compassion. On the other hand, the elder son is like so

> many who try to serve God in religious practice but misunderstand his great love. Rather than accepting God's unmerited grace and fostering a close relationship of trust, they try to earn divine favor. The compassionate father is the key player and leading actor throughout the drama. He loves the rebel who plays the role of a sinner despised by all. But the father also loves the religious son who is every bit as much a sinner as his rebellious brother. He is a respectable sinner, but surprisingly, his needs turn out to be very like those of his brother. Whether one has deep religious convictions or rejects faith in God altogether, the divine compassion is the same. The needs of both lost sons are met by the compassion of the father. [147]

Without doubt, the most important truth in all creation, in fact, in eternity, is the LOVE OF GOD! Why is God's love that important? Nancy Missler does a masterful job of answering that question. Thus, we will quote extensively from her as a fitting climax on the practical importance of love: [148]

> "Why does everyone make such a big issue about God's Love? What's so special about it? Why is it so important? There is only one answer to these questions. 1 John 4:8 says, God is Agape. This is why Agape-Love is so special, so important, and why we are commanded to seek it with all of our heart, mind and soul. Here are 5-reasons why God's love is important to have and pass on to others:
>
> 1. **HAVING GOD'S LOVE IN OUR LIVES IS THE WHOLE MEANING AND PURPOSE OF OUR CHRISTIAN WALK.**
> The Bible says that God has called us to be Christians for two primary reasons: To love Him, and then to love others. (Matthew 22:37) We were not called to be

"Christians" just to be happy and content within ourselves, but to be vessels and channels of God's Love-experiencing His Love first-hand, and then passing it on to others.

1 Timothy 1:5 says, Agape is the goal of our instruction and the fulfillment of all of God's Word in us! In other words, the Bible is summed up in our personally knowing and passing on God's Love!

1 Corinthians 13:1-3 says, "Though I speak with the tongues of men and of angels, and have not [Agape], I am become as a sounding brass, or a tinkling cymbal. And though I have the gift of prophecy, and understand all mysteries and all knowledge; and though I have all faith, so that I could remove mountains, and have not [Agape], I am nothing. And though I bestow all my goods to feed the poor, and though I give my body to be burned, and have not [Agape], it profiteth me nothing."

God is saying that without His Love, all the intellectual knowledge in the world, all the supernatural understanding in the world, and all the faith in the world will profit and benefit us nothing. Without His Love, we will still be empty, lonely and without meaning or purpose in our lives. Love is the reason God created us in the first place. And, thus, if we don't learn to love and be loved in the way God intends, we will have wasted our lives.

Many people recognize this far too late. After working hard their entire lives to reach their "own" aspired goals (to be happy, to have their own business, to have financial independence, etc.), they realize that in the process of attaining these things, they have lost the true meaning of their lives, which is love. Some of these people attained everything materially that anyone could ever possibly want, and yet they personally still remain empty and unfulfilled. Many "successful" business leaders will admit that they would give anything to be able to live their lives over again. If they had a second chance, many say, they would be careful not to miss the most important thing in their life, which is love and relationships.

A newspaper article, written many years ago, told the story of a very wealthy and famous gentleman. Throughout his life, he thought love and relationships were just a nuisance and a deterrent to what "success" was all about. He thus determined to amass a fortune and make a name for himself. He certainly did both. But in the process, he lost all his relationships. And, in the end, when he was too old to work, he sat night after night, alone in his huge, empty mansion, filled with priceless-and yet worthless-possessions. He had missed the very reason he was created-to love and be loved.

Edgar Jackson wrote an excellent book called "Understanding Loneliness". He shares that psychologists have now exchanged the word "identity" for the word "love." Love is our true-identity and purpose. Without love we will be lost, despite all the fortune, power, prestige, and education we amass. Love must be the supreme and central issue of our lives or we will die psychologically, socially, spiritually, and even physically. Christianity is unique, in that it is a religion of Love. Christianity has the answers that everyone is so desperate for-

Jesus Christ is Love (1 John 4:8). God has called us, as believers, to be His co-workers, His co-laborers, and His partners in spreading His gospel of Love to others. Our lives as Christians, then, are not just something to be enjoyed or to derive happiness from, but an opportunity to be an open vessel for God's Love. God has called us specifically for this purpose! 1 John 3:14 says, "He that loveth not... abideth in death." This means, if we are not loving, we are dying! We're dying because we are separated from the true meaning of our lives, which is Love.

2. **GOD'S LOVE IS IMPORTANT IN OUR LIVES BECAUSE IT IS THE ONLY WAY OTHERS WILL KNOW THAT WE ARE TRUE CHRISTIANS.**

By this shall all men know that ye are My disciples, if ye have love one to another (John 13:35).

As we look around us-at our churches, our families, our friends, and our kids-we see that many are dying from a lack of love. Many of them are caught up in the "do's and don'ts" of Scripture, the prophecies, the gifts, the healings, the miracles, the "work" of faith, the signs and wonders, etc., but where is God's Love? Scripture says, "They will know we are Christians by our Love." Where is God's Love today? How can we be Spirit filled and yet not Love filled? To me, they're the very same thing! God's Love is simply the glue that holds everything together. And, it's missing!

1 John 2:4 says, "He that saith 'I know Him,' [I am a Christian], and keepeth not His commandments, [to love one another] is a liar, and the truth is not in him." God's Love doesn't just "fall out of heaven."

His Love must come through us. We are extensions of God's Love to one another. God just needs a willing body-arms and legs-to pour His Love through.

Larry Crabb, in his book, "Inside Out," shares that Christians can spend years in the Bible developing a real love for the truth; but, he says, if they come away without knowing God in a deeper and more real way and without His Love for people, then they will have wasted their time. The whole purpose of Bible is to make us more loving, not more scholarly.

David Needham, in his excellent book: "Birthright: Christian, Do You Know Who You Are?" confirms this same thought. "... the big task is not the finding of the truth, but the living of it!" To me, this says it all! It's only Jesus' Love through us-in our actions-that will bring our families, our husbands, our children, our neighbors, and our bosses to the feet of Jesus. Since God is Love, the only way these people will know that we are, indeed, Christians is by the "real" Love that comes from us.

1 Peter 4:8 says, "Above all things have fervent Love among yourselves; for Love, shall cover the multitude of sins." This simply means that if we hear something bad about a brother, if we are walking in true Agape, we will take it no further. We will take it to the Lord first, pray about it, and, if need be, go to that brother to find out the truth, but real Love will not pass that sin on to another (gossip).

A nonbeliever said to me recently, "I really don't want to go to that church anymore because the people there are just a bunch of phonies. I work with 'so and so' (a church goer) and you should see what he does during the rest of the week! How can he call himself a Christian?"

It's interesting to me that nonbelievers know the "real thing" when they see it. They can spot the "phonies" a mile away. I find this fascinating, since we ourselves are often fooled by our so-called "brothers and sisters." So often God must combat, not only unbelief in a person, but also unravel all the damage other "so-called" Christians have done. When asked what the greatest obstacle to Christianity in India was, Mahatma Gandhi answered, "Other Christians."

It's only God's genuine love through us that can truly touch another's life and bring them to Jesus. Our flowery and empty words about Jesus are not enough. Our actions must match our words in order for it to be truth. In other words, we need to "live His Love."

3. GOD'S LOVE IS ALSO IMPORTANT BECAUSE IT PROVES WE ARE ABIDING IN GOD.

John 15 is a wonderful chapter-totally devoted to what it means to abide in God. It says that abiding in God is simply staying in His Love and remaining in His Presence. Continually presenting our wills and lives to Him, so that He can use us to pass His Love on to others.

A Greek scholar friend of ours, who studied The Way of Agape, pointed out to me that the word "to bear" in John 15:2 could be translated "to carry fruit from one location to another." In other words, God wants us to be an open channel, carrying His Love on to others. He also suggests that the phrase "abide in

Me" or "remain in Me" could also be translated "rest in My Love." If this is true, then God's promise in verse 7 makes much more sense. If we continue to "rest in His Love" (i.e., continue to be an open channel), then we can ask whatever we will and He will do it.

As we said before, the proof that we are Christians does not come through our knowledge of Scripture, from our spiritual gifts or even our church attendance, but only by how much of God's Love we are sharing. John 15:14 says that if we are obedient and do what God commands (remain in His Love and carry fruit) then we will be His "friends." Abraham is a good example of someone who rested in and remained in God's Love. Thus, Abraham is remembered in Scripture as a "friend of God" and one who "walked with God." Abraham had that intimate relationship with God that we all desire. Staying in, remaining in, and resting in God's Love is the only way to achieve that union.

4. **LOVING WITH GOD'S LOVE IS IMPORTANT BECAUSE IT SHOWS THAT WE ARE FILLED WITH THE "FULLNESS OF GOD".**

The fullness of God is experiencing His Life-His Supernatural Love, Wisdom and Power-though us, in place of our own. It is God's Character, His Image and His Fullness that we are passing on, not our own.

Ephesians 3:19 says we are "to know the Love of Christ, which passeth knowledge, that ye might be filled with all the fullness of God." Stephen, in Acts 6-7, is a wonderful example of being filled with the "fullness of God." Even when the elders and the high priests persecuted him and charged him falsely before the Sanhedrin, he was still visibly "full of faith and power" (6:8). Thus, the people who saw him, "were not able to resist the wisdom by which he spoke." They "saw his face as it had been the face of an angel" (Acts 6:10, 15). Then in Acts 7:60, as they were stoning him, Stephen said, "Lord, lay not this sin to their charge." Steven, at the moment they were stoning him to death, was still so "full of the Holy Spirit" (verse 55), that he could unconditionally forgive and love them.

2 Corinthians 4:7,10-12 says, "But we have this treasure in earthen vessels, that the excellency of the power may be of God, and not of us... Always bearing about in the body the dying of the Lord Jesus, [so] that the life also of Jesus might be made manifest in our body. For we which live are always delivered unto death for Jesus' sake, that the life also of Jesus might be made manifest in our mortal flesh. So, then death worketh in us, but life in you."

5. GOD'S LOVE IS IMPORTANT BECAUSE IT'S THE PERFECT 'BOND OF UNION' BETWEEN GOD AND ME, AND OTHERS AND ME.

Colossians 3:14 says, "And above all these put-on love, which binds everything together in perfect harmony" (ESV).

God's Love not only initiates a relationship and maintains that relationship, it also continually reconciles that relationship. God's Love is the only power that enables us to unconditionally forgive and forget what others have done to us. When God cleanses and heals us by His Love, our wounds are not just buried and pushed down-continuing to unconsciously motivate our actions-they are literally removed from us. As God says in Psalms 103:12, "As far as the east is from the west, So, far hath He removed our transgressions [our sins] from us."

I heard a Christian radio psychologist once say to a man whose wife had just left him, "You just forgive and forget what others have done to you and go on as if nothing ever happened." Have you ever tried to do that in your own power? It's a total impossibility! On our own, how can we rid ourselves of all the hurts and wounds we have unjustly sustained by others? There's no way we can! There is no way we can naturally forgive another person, and go on in that relationship "as if nothing had ever happened," unless of course, we bury our real feelings, build walls and become totally desensitized.

Many people live this way because they don't realize they have another option. They don't realize that by having Jesus in their hearts, He not only will heal and remove their wounds and hurts, but also, He will give them the love they need to genuinely go on as if nothing has ever happened. Only God's Love can cleanse us, heal us, and enable us to forgive others. Only His Love can reconcile us. Only His Love will wipe away our divisions and our discords. And only His Love will unite us as one!" [149]

KNOWING THE FATHER'S HEART

"The glory that you have given me I have given to them, that they may be one even as we are one, I in them and you in me, that they may become perfectly one, so that the world may know that you sent me and loved them even as you loved me. Father, I desire that they also, whom you have given me, may be with me where I am, to see my glory that you have given me because you loved me before the foundation of the world. O righteous Father, even though the world does not know you, I know you, and these know that you have sent me. I made known to them your name, and I will continue to make it known, that the love with which you have loved me may be in them, and I in them."

~ John 17:22-26 ESV

"GOD IS LOVE"
~ 1 John 4:8

It was his home now. But it could not be his home till he had gone from it and returned to it. Now he was the Prodigal Son. — G.K. Chesterton

KNOWING THE FATHER'S HEART

STUDY QUESTIONS (Part-2)

From: *A PARABLE IS...*

1. What is a parable?
2. Approximately how many parables are there in the New Testament Gospels?

From: *THERE WAS A MAN:*

3. The Bible is essentially (fill in the blank)?
4. When the younger son said "give me..." it was like saying (what – fill in the blank)?
5. Man's declaration of independence from God always results in (what – fill in the blank)?
6. Explain the difference between man-made religion and true religion.
7. What does Torrance mean by: "there is no God behind the back of Jesus Christ"?
8. St. Symeon the New Theologian said this about love and creation: "Apart from love (fill in the blank).

From: *FATHER'S APPARENT INACTION:*

9. What two things does the apparent inaction of the father reveal?
10. However unreasonable and absurd it is for free moral agents to turn away from a loving God, (what: fill in the

blank) makes it possible because (what: fill in the blank) is always a choice and therefore its (what: fill in the blank) creates the opposite (what: fill in the blank).

From: *JESUS IS GOD FROM GOD:*

11. If we are loved and chosen of Jesus the Son, then we are loved and chosen of (who – fill in the blank)?

From: *THE NICENE CREED:*

12. The one thing that the Arian Christ cannot communicate to humanity is (what – fill in the blank)?
13. According to Dragas, "God is uncreated in the Father, but He is (fill in the blank) in the Son."
14. Torrance said, "the incarnation was the coming of God to save us (fill in the blank) where humanity is at its wickedest in its enmity and violence against (fill in the blank).
15. Jesus joined Adam (fill in the blank) and by His perfect obedience, bent the human will back to God for us and (fill in the blank).

From: *INTO A FAR COUNTRY:*

16. The parable of the prodigal son reads like (fill in the blank).
17. N.T. Wright says, "the gospel is not an account of how people get saved. The Gospel is (what – fill in the blank)?
18. To be "lost" means to be (fill in the blank). Explain.

From: *O HAPPY FAULT:*

19. Briefly explain the theological concept of *Felix culpa?*

KNOWING THE FATHER'S HEART

From: *UNDERSTANDING GOD'S LOVE-WRATH:*

20. Historian Perry Miller suggests that America's Enlightenment began and ended with (who – fill in the blank)?
21. Edwards rightly said that "all the virtue that is saving and that distinguishes true Christians from others, is summed up in (what – fill in the blank)?
22. St. Maximus the Confessor said: "Every soul that, despite God's admonitions, deliberately cleaves to (what – fill in the blank), hardens like clay and drives itself to (what – fill in the blank)?

From: *LOVE MUST BE FREE:*

23. Kallistos (Timothy) Ware said: "It is natural for God to be (fill in the blank) as it is to be (fill in the blank). Explain.
24. In the second century Letter to Diognetus, it says that God will to save man by (what – fill in the blank), and not (what – fill in the blank).
25. Is death a curse from God? Explain.
26. Fr. Morelli says, "we are not sinners in the hands of an angry God, but rather sinners (fill in the blank)?

From: *COMBATING THE RELIGIOUS SPIRIT:*

27. Jesus' main battle was with whom?
28. What does the Bible mean by saying that the Pharisee stood by himself praying?

From: *THE TALE OF TWO PRODIGALS:*

29. What does the author mean that in this parable: "the lost is found and the found is lost"?

30. What was Jesus talking about when He said… *"We played the pipe for you, but you did not dance." "We sang a dirge, and you did not cry."*?

From: *GOD'S STEADFAST MERCY:*

31. What was the motivation for Jesus' ministry actions? Explain.

From: *CONCEPTIONS OF THE AFTERLIFE:*

32. What is one of the most enduring depictions of hell in the Western Church? Explain.
33. C.S. Lewis and N.T. Wright see hell as what (fill in the blank)?
34. George MacDonald views heaven as (what – fill in the blank) and hell as (what – fill in the blank).
35. In C.S. Lewis "The Great Divorce," what size is "the gray city"? Explain.

From: *DEFINING PERSONHOOD:*

36. William G. T. Shedd argues that personality does not develop or exist in (what – fill in the blank), but only in (what – fill in the blank)?
37. Briefly explain the *"Gesasah Ceremony"* in relation to the returning prodigal?
38. Briefly explain what the author calls the *"scandal of grace"*?

From: *THE RUNNING FATHER:*

39. Did the returning prodigal have a repentant motivation for coming home? Explain.

KNOWING THE FATHER'S HEART

From: *THE BEMA SEAT:*

40. What does it mean that "love is its own reward"?
41. Love is the measure of (fill in the blank). Self-centeredness is the measure of all (fill in the blank).
42. What did Paul mean in Galatians 5:6 that "faith works by love"?

From: *THE GLORIOUS GOSPEL:*

43. Write out the meaning of the Gospel according to William Tyndale?
44. Explain what the Gospel is NOT...
45. Explain what the Gospel IS...

From: *IT IS FINISHED:*

46. What does the word "tetelestai" mean?
47. Contrast legal repentance and evangelical repentance.

From: *AVOIDING EXTREMES:*

48. Too live under true grace is to be empowered to (what – fill in the blank).
49. Contrast antinomianism (hyper-grace) and legalism (Pharisee-ism)?

From: *WELCOME HOME:*

50. What was the perennial hope of Israel?

From: *GRACIOUS GIFTS OF GOD:*

51. Alexander Maclaren said: *I question whether forgiveness is ever true which is not, like God's...* (fill in the blank).

52. List the three gifts of the father to the prodigal and explain their spiritual significance.

From: *MAKING IT PRACTICAL:*

53. Comment briefly on each of the 5-reasons stated for the primacy of God's love.

From: *GENERAL QUESTIONS:*

54. What were several significant things you learned from this course?
55. How could this course be improved?

PARTIAL BIBLIOGRAPHY:

Baker, Mark. D. Proclaiming the Scandal of the Cross: Contemporary Images of the Atonement. Grand Rapids: Baker Academic. 2006.

Barclay, William Barclay. The Parables of Jesus. Westminster John Knox Press. 1999.

Barth, Karl. Church Dogmatics. Volume 2. The Doctrine of Reconciliation. Part 1. 2004.

Berkhof, Louis. Systematic Theology. Grand Rapids: WM. B. Eerdmans publishing co. 1939.

Calvin, John. Institutes of the Christian Religion. Grand Rapids: WM B. Eerdmans publishing co. Originally written: 1536. Current edition: 1995.

Channing, William E. The Works of William E. Channing, "The Moral Argument Against Calvinism," (Boston: American Unitarian Association), 1889.

Cross. F.L. Livingstone, E.A. editors (1974). "Circumincession." The Oxford Dictionary of the Christian Church (2nd edition). Oxford: Oxford University Press.

Dragas, George (editor). The Eternal Son in T.F. Torrance, The Incarnation: Ecumenical Studies in the Nicene-Constantinopolitan Creed AD 381. The Handsel Press. 1981. Reprint: Wipf & Stock.

Fairbairn, Donald. Life in the Trinity (An introduction to theology with the help of the Church Fathers). Downers Grove: IL. InterVarsity Press. 2009.

Irenaeus, Against Heresies 3.18.1 in A. Roberts and J. Donaldson (eds), The Writings of Irenaeus Vol. 1 (Edinburgh: T & T Clark, 1848).

Keller, Tim. The Reason for God: Belief in an Age of Skepticism. Dutton Penguin Publishers. 2008.

Kesich, Veselin. The First Day of the New Creation: The Resurrection and the Christian Faith." Yonkers NY: St Vladimir's Seminary Press. 1997.

Lewis C.S. The Great Divorce. HarperOne Publishing. Revised: 2015.

Lewis C.S. Mere Christianity. HarperOne Publishing. Revised 2015.

Liddell, Henry and Scott, Robert. A Greek-English Lexicon. Originally published: 1843. Oxford University Press.

Louw, J.P. Nida, Eugene A. (editors). Greek-English Lexicon of the New Testament. 2-Volume set. United Bible Society. 1999.

Osbeck, Kenneth W. 101 More Hymn Stories. Grand Rapids: Kregel. 1965.

Prestige, G. Leonard. God in Patristic Thought. SPCK. 1964.

Richardson, Cyril C. (editor). Early Christian Fathers. NY: Macmillan Publishing Co. 1970.

Schweitzer, Albert. The Mysticism of Paul the Apostle, Johns Hopkins University Press. Reprinted 1998.

Snyder Belousek, Darrin W. Atonement, Justice, and Peace: The Message of the Cross and the Mission of Church. Grand Rapids: William B. Eerdmans Publishing. 2012.

Stiller, Brian C. Preaching Parables to Post moderns. (Fortress Resources for Preaching). Augsburg Fortress Publishers. 2005.

Torrance, Thomas F. The Christian Doctrine of God; One Being Three Persons. Bloomsbury T & T Clark. Reprint 2001.

Torrance, Thomas F. The Mediation of Christ. Helmers & Howard Publishers. Revised 1992.

Van der Borght, Eddy A.J.G. The Unity of the Church: A Theological State of the Art and Beyond. Brill Publishers. Leiden (Netherlands). 2010.

Walker, Robert (Editor). Incarnation: The Person and Life of Christ, by Thomas F. Torrance. IVP Academic. Reprinted 2015.

Wallis, Jim. The Call to Conversion: why faith is always personal but never private. HarperOne. 1981.

Ware, Kallistos (Timothy). The Orthodox Church. 1963. London: Penguin Books.

Wright, N.T. What Saint Paul really said. Grand Rapids: MI: WM. B. Eerdmans. 1997.

RECOMMENDED READING:

Fairbairn, Donald. Life in the Trinity (An introduction to theology with the help of the Church Fathers). Downers Grove: IL. InterVarsity Press. 2009.

Keller, Tim. The Reason for God: Belief in an Age of Skepticism. Dutton Penguin Publishers. 2008.

Lewis C.S. The Great Divorce. HarperOne Publishing. Revised: 2015.

Lewis C.S. Mere Christianity. HarperOne Publishing. Revised 2015.

Torrance, Thomas F. The Mediation of Christ. Helmers & Howard Publishers. Revised 1992.

Torrance, Thomas F. The Christian Doctrine of God; One Being Three Persons. Bloomsbury T & T Clark. Reprint 2001.

Wright, N.T. What Saint Paul really said. Grand Rapids: MI: WM. B. Eerdmans. 1997.

ENDNOTES:

FROM THE *GENERAL INTRODUCTION:*

[1] Catechism: a summary of the principles of Christian religion in the form of questions and answers, used for the instruction of Christians.

[2] Source: Alan Carr. http://www.sermonnotebook.org/new%20testament/Lk%2015_11-24.htm (accessed 12.09.16).

[3] The author wishes to express sincere thanks to Alan Carr (www.sermonnotebook.org) for this excellent outline re: The Prodigal Son Parable. It is indeed, a helpful resource to the Body of Christ!

[4] Source: sacerdotus.wordpress.com (accessed 07.31.16).

[5] Source: http://www.rembrandtpainting.net/rembrandt's_prodigal_son.html (accessed 06.24.16).

[6] In the public domain.

[7] Altar calls (so called) are actually a rather recent historic phenomenon, only beginning in the late 1800s. Another early name for them was the "anxious seat". The term (as such) is not found in the Bible, but is an attempt to adapt the call for repentance to particular cultural context, where such a public show of confession may find greater response. One of the most famous 19th century revivalists; Charles G. Finney, "popularized the idea of the 'altar call' in order to sign up his converts for the abolition movement." (Source: Wallis, Jim

(January 1981). The Call to Conversion: Why Faith Is Always Personal but Never Private. HarperOne. p. 78.)

[8] "Vladimir, Prince of Kiev, is a pagan playboy with a harem of eight hundred. He is cruel and powerful, subjugating much of the region known as Rus to himself. Ignoring the increase of Christianity among his subjects, he has erected many statues to his people's ancient gods. However, Prince Vladimir begins to recognize that pagan gods are unable to unify Rus. Becoming interested in the question of faith while planning a campaign against the Eastern Roman Empire, he has sent embassies to the neighboring states of Bulgaria, Khazar, and Byzantium to examine their beliefs. The ambassadors return, declaring that the Islam of Bulgaria is too unhappy a religion to adopt. The fact that Islam bans fermented drink and pork does not set well with the Russians, who cannot imagine life without either—especially the drink. Vladimir himself rejects the Judaism of his Khazar neighbors, for he says the Jewish loss of Jerusalem and its temple proves that God has forsaken them. As for German Catholicism, the ambassadors describe it as plain and dour. Their impression of the faith of their Orthodox neighbors to the south is altogether different, however. Upon attending a service at the glorious Hagia Sophia cathedral in Constantinople, they report:"

> And we went into the Greek lands, and we were led into a place where they serve their God, and we did not know where we were, on heaven or on earth; and do not know how to tell about this. All we know is that God lives there with people and their service is better than in any other country. We cannot forget that beauty since each person, if he eats something sweet, will not take something bitter afterwards; so we cannot remain any more in paganism.

KNOWING THE FATHER'S HEART

Source: Christian History Institute. https://www.christianhistoryinstitute.org/incontext/article/vladimir/ (accessed 07.28.16).

[9] The Trinity (Russian: Троица, tr. Troitsa) also called The Hospitality of Abraham in this icon created by a Russian painter Andrei Rublev in the 15th century. The icon depicts the three angels who visited Abraham at the Oak of Mamre (Genesis 18:1–8), but the painting is full of symbolism and is interpreted as an icon of the Holy Trinity.

[10] The icon of The Troitsa Holy Trinity which depicts the Godhead seated at the communion table of fellowship.

[11] To appreciate what Paul is saying, we need to understand what that phrase "in Christ" means. There is a key phrase that runs through Paul's epistles. If we were to take this phrase out of these writings, there would be very little left of Paul's exposition of the gospel. This recurring phrase, which is the central theme of Paul's theology, is the expression, "in Christ" or "in Christ Jesus." Now this phrase is sometimes expressed by other similar phrases, that is, "in Him" or "by Him" or "through Him" or "in the Beloved" or "together with Him" or "in whom." These are all synonymous terms applying to the "in Christ" motif or idea.

[12] Albert Schweitzer. The Mysticism of Paul the Apostle, Johns Hopkins University Press. Reprinted 1998. Page 380.

[13] Source of Greek chart below: http://www.ntgreek.org/learn_nt_greek/inter-tense.htm (accessed 07.19.16).

Tense Name	Kind of Action	Time Element (In Indicative Mood)
Present	Progressive (or 'Continuous')	present
Aorist	Simple (or 'Summary') Occurrence	past
Perfect	Completed, with Results	past, with present results
Imperfect	Progressive (or 'Continuous')	past
Future	Simple Occurrence	future
Past Perfect	Completed, with Results	past
Future Perfect	Completed, with Results	future

Kind of Action and Time of Action for Each Verb Tense

[14] εὐφρανθῶμεν (euphranthōmen) [pronounced (yoo-fran-tho-men]. Source: Bible hub. http://biblehub.com/greek/euphrantho_men_2165.htm (accessed 06.24.16).

FROM PART-ONE:
(Theological implications of Divine Love)

[15] Source of this picture: http://feast.icej.org/content/dancing-streets-jerusalem (accessed 07.28.16).

[16] Source: http://theodorakis.net/orthodoxquotescomplete.html (accessed 07.01.16).

[17] Source: www.playitbyeardrama.com (accessed 07.31.16).

[18] Source: MacLaren's Expositions. http://biblehub.com/commentaries/zephaniah/3-17.htm (accessed 07.01.16).

[19] Source: jorgeschulz.wordpress.com (accessed 07.19.16).

[20] Source: THE OVERFLOWING FELLOWSHIP. https://jorgeschulz.wordpress.com/tag/perichoresis/ (accessed 08.01.16).

²¹ Greek: περιχώρησις (transliterated: perikhōrēsis, sometimes spelled – perichoresis).

²² Prestige, G.L. God in Patristic Thought SPCK (1964) p. 291.

²³ Cross, F.L.; Livingstone, E.A., eds. (1974). "Circumincession". The Oxford Dictionary of the Christian Church (2 ed.). Oxford: Oxford University Press.

²⁴ Liddell and Scott (Greek–English Lexicon), s.v. I-III.

²⁵ Douglas Kelly, author and theologian, defines the doctrine of *perichoresis* in this way, *"Father, Son, and Holy Spirit inhere in one another and coexist, entirely, and perfectly in one another, so that where one is, the others are, and what one is involved in doing, the others are also involved in doing"*. Source: Douglas Kelly, Systematic Theology Course Study Guide. Page 40. https://theblessedrebellion.wordpress.com/2011/06/15/doctrine-of-trinitarian-perichoresis-pt-1/ (accessed 06.24.16).

²⁶ Source: http://trinityinyou.com/welcome-to-trinity-in-you/19-2/ (accessed 11.28.16).

²⁷ Source: google-images.

²⁸ "Aristotle's account of motion can be found in the Physics. By motion, Aristotle (384-322 B.C.E.) understands any kind of change. He defines motion as the actuality of a potentiality. Initially, Aristotle's definition seems to involve a contradiction. However, commentators on the works of Aristotle, such as St. Thomas Aquinas, maintain that this is the only way to define motion." (Source): http://www.iep.utm.edu/aris-mot/ (accessed 07.28.16).

[29] The first evidence based atomic theory was by presented by English chemist, physicist, John Dalton in the early 1800s.

[30] Source: Jonathan Marlowe. https://musicanddancing.wordpress.com/perichoresis/ (accessed 06.24.16).

[31] Source: Elmer Colyer. https://musicanddancing.wordpress.com/perichoresis/ (accessed 07.01.16).

[32] Source: Leonard Sweet "Dancing with God." http://goodnewsmag.org/2013/09/dancing-with-god/ (accessed 07.01.16).

[33] The phase "in the bosom" (κολπον kolpos) in this context conveys the eternal intimate communion between the Father and Son. Most bibles, even some paraphrases, do not alter the word "bosom" probably because our English vernacular still uses the word to express the seat of deep affection. Albert Barnes commentary notes on this verse reads: "In the bosom of the Father" as an expression taken from the custom among the Orientals of reclining at their meals.

[34] Source: Taken from the book by Tim Keller entitled: The Reason for God: Belief in an Age of Skepticism: http://greatexchange.tumblr.com/post/51223403352/the-dance-of-god-tim-keller-on-the-trinity (accessed 07.01.16).

[35] Source: jorgeschulz.wordpress.com (accessed 07.19.16).

[36] Source: David Lomas, The Truest Thing about You: Identity, Desire, and Why It All Matters.

37 The words of this familiar hymn were penned by Carrie Breck and set to music by Grant Tuller. For details, see Kenneth W. Osbeck, 101 More Hymn Stories (Grand Rapids: Kregel, 1965), 85-88.

38 Greek: Ἐν ἀρχῇ ἦν ὁ Λόγος, καὶ ὁ Λόγος ἦν πρὸς τὸν Θεόν, καὶ Θεὸς ἦν ὁ Λόγος. Transliteration: "En (in the) archē (beginning) ho (the) Logos (Word) kai (and) ho (the) Logos (Word) ēn (was) pros (with) ton Theon (God) kai (and) Theos (God) ēn (was) ho (the) Logos (Word)." Source: http://biblehub.com/text/john/1-1.htm (accessed 06.22.16).

39 Source: ICHTHYS. http://ichthys.com/mail-John%201-1.htm (accessed 06.22.16).

40 This is one of the most common verses of contention between the Jehovah's Witnesses and Christians. Their false assumption is that Jesus is not God in flesh but Michael the archangel who became a man. Therefore, since they deny that Jesus is divine, they have altered the Bible in John 1:1 so that Jesus is not divine in nature. The New World Translation has added the word "a" to the verse so it says, " . . . and the Word was a god." SOURCE: http://carm.org/religious-movements/jehovahs-witnesses/john-11-word-was-god (accessed 06.22.16).

41 In verse one of John 1:1-3, the clause "the Word was God" cannot legitimately be translated "the Word was a God". First, earlier in the verse, the apostle John had used the definite article with the Greek word *theos* to refer to the Father according to customary usage ("the [sc. Father] God"), and so to use the identical combination again to refer to the Word would be potentially confusing, making it seem as if "the Word" was really identical to "the [sc. Father] God", one of the very points that John is disproving here. Secondly, Greek does not possess an indefinite article ("a/an"), but it does have an indefinite

pronoun ("a certain one"; Greek *tis*) – which is the very word that a Greek reader would expect here if the point was that Christ was somehow a god, but not really "God". So John only had three ways to write this: (1) the Word was "the God" (but this would mean that there was no real distinction between the Father and Christ); (2) the Word was "a certain god" (but this would mean that Christ was a lesser sort of divinity, not God on the level of the Father) (this is the interpretation of the Jehovah's Witness); or (3) the Word was "God" – which is what John actually wrote, thus fully and unambiguously attributing deity to the Word (Logos) as distinct from the Father. SOURCE: ICHTHYS. http://ichthys.com/mail-John%201-1.htm (accessed 06.22.16).

[42] A quote from the Nicene Creed.

[43] Source: Christian History Institute. https://www.christianhistoryinstitute.org/uploaded/50ae4a184e3b66.49033776.pdf (accessed 06.22.16).

[44] Source: adapted by the book review of "The First Day of the New Creation: The Resurrection and the Christian Faith", by Veselin Kesich. Yonkers NY: St Vladimir's Seminary Press. 1997.
https://www.amazon.com/First-Day-New-Creation-Resurrection/dp/0913836788

[45] Sermon by Fr Luke Veronis "Be Renewed in Christ" (February 4, 2016). Source: http://myocn.net/sermon-the-new-man-in-christ/ (accessed 07.28.16).

[46] A quote from "Proclaiming the Scandal of the Cross: Contemporary Images of the Atonement" by Mark D. Baker. Grand Rapids: Baker Academic. Pages 99-100. 2006.

[47] Mere Christianity, by C.S. Lewis.

[48] Irenaeus, Against Heresies 3.18.1 in A. Roberts and J. Donaldson (eds), The Writings of Irenaeus Vol. 1 (Edinburgh: T & T Clark, 1848), p. 337-338

[49] A collection of quotes attributed to Spanish mystic and Carmelite nun; Saint Teresa of Avila (1515-1582). http://ocarm.org/en/content/ocarm/teresa-avila-quotes (accessed 07.01.16).

[50] Philippians 2:3-11 NKJV.

[51] Supporting scriptures: Proverbs 18:12; Matthew 5:3–10; 6:19–21; 19:27–30; 20:26–27; Mark 10:42–45; Luke 6:38; 9:23–24; John 12:25.

[52] Source: https://bible.org/seriespage/6-work-your-way-down-ladder-philippians-25-11 (accessed 06.23.16).

[53] Source: http://www.relevantmagazine.com/life/whole-life/success-upside-down-kingdom (accessed 07.01.16).

[54] Source: http://www.pravoslavie.ru/english/print43906.htm (accessed 07.28.16).

[55] The following is a brief contrast/comparison between Calvinism, Arminianism, and Trinitarian Theology. The following is an extended quote from Grace Communion International from their website on this important conversation:

CALVINISM – is a theology that developed from the teachings of the Protestant reformer John Calvin (1509-1564). Calvinism emphasizes the sovereignty of God's will in election and salvation. Most Calvinists define God's "elect" as a subset of the human race; Christ died for only some people ("limited" or "particular" atonement"). Those elect for whom he did die, however, were truly and effectively saved in the finished work of Christ, long before they became aware of it and accepted it. According to Calvinist doctrine, it is inevitable that those Christ died for will come to faith in him at some point. This is called "irresistible grace."

Trinitarian theology's main disagreement with Calvinism is over the scope of reconciliation. Its objection is based on the fundamental fact of who Jesus is and that he is one in will, purpose, mind, authority and act with the Father in the Spirit. The whole God is Savior and Jesus is the new Adam who died for all. The Bible asserts that Christ made atonement "not only for our sins, but for the sins of the whole world" (1 John 2:2). And while Trinitarian theology rejects the restrictive extent of "limited atonement" and the determinism of "irresistible grace," it agrees with Calvinism that forgiveness, reconciliation, redemption, justification, etc. were all accomplished effectively by what Christ did. And these gospel truths have been secured for us irrespective of our response to them.

ARMINIANISM – derives from the teachings of another Protestant reformer, Jacob Arminius (1560-1609). Arminius insisted that Jesus died for all humanity, and that all people can be saved if they take necessary, personal action, which is enabled by the Spirit. This theology, while not ignoring God's sovereignty, gives a more central or key role to human decision and free will. Its premise is that salvation, forgiveness, reconciliation, redemption, justification, etc., are not actually effective unless a person has faith. For only if God foresees a person using their free choice to receive Christ, does he then elect them. Those whom he foresees rejecting his salvation, he condemns. So like the Calvinist, in the end God wills the salvation of some and the condemnation of others.

TRINITARIAN THEOLOGY – differs from Arminianism over the effectiveness of the reconciliation. Atonement, or "at-one-ment" between God and humanity, is only a hypothetical possibility for Arminians; it does not become an accomplished actuality unless God foresees someone's decision of faith. In this view, God, on the basis of his foreknowledge of an individual's acceptance or rejection, then accepts or rejects that person. Trinitarian theology, however, teaches that the atonement and reconciliation represents the heart and mind of God towards all and is objectively true in Christ, even before it has been subjectively accepted and experienced and remains true even if some deny it. God has one ultimate will or purpose for all, realized from the Father, through the Son and in the Spirit.

While Calvinism and Arminianism emphasize different aspects of salvation theology, Trinitarian theology has attempted, as did Church Fathers Irenaeus, Athanasius, and Gregory, to maintain in harmony the wideness of God's love emphasized by Arminians with the unconditional faithfulness of God emphasized by Calvinists. Incarnational, Trinitarian theology aligns neither with traditional Calvinism nor Arminianism. It emphasizes the sovereignty of God's Triune holy love that calls for our response. His sovereign will is expressed in accord with God's being a fellowship of holy love. Its center is the heart, mind, character and nature of God revealed in the Person and Work of Jesus Christ, the Incarnate Savior and Redeemer. God's sovereignty is most clearly and profoundly shown in Jesus Christ. The place and importance of human response to God's grace is also shown in Jesus Christ who makes a perfect and free response to God in our place and on our behalf as our Great High Priest. Our response then is a gift given by the Holy Spirit by which we share in Christ's perfect response for us in our place and on our behalf.

[56] CCBI does not espouse 5-point (federal, classic) Calvinism. We consider ourselves modified, evangelical Calvinists (Trinitarian), as explained throughout this text.

[57] Chart (source): www.reformedresources.com/au (accessed 07.28.16).

[58] Source of these pictures: google-images (accessed 07.31.16).

[59] For a general introduction to Trinitarian Theology, please visit: https://www.gci.org/theology (accessed 07.19.16).

[60] Source: Grace Communion International. https://www.gci.org/CO/election (accessed 07.01.16). John Webster, Barth: Outstanding Christian Thinkers (Continuum, 2000), 91.

[61] Ibid. Grace Communion International in commenting and quoting from about the theology of Karl Barth. Karl Barth, Dogmatics in Outline (Harper & Row: 1959). Karl Barth, Church Dogmatics II/2 (T&T Clark, 2004). Karl Barth, Church Dogmatics IV/1(T & T Clark, 1956).

[62] Karl Barth, Church Dogmatics II/2 (page 140.)

[63] Source: Patheos. http://www.patheos.com/blogs/rogereolson/2013/03/was-karl-barth-a-universalist-a-new-look-at-an-old-question/ (accessed 07.01.16).

[64] Church father Origen, believed and taught that without *"apokatastasis,"* God would be less than fully God. This doctrine was condemned at The Second Council of Constantinople, which is the Fifth Ecumenical Council.

⁶⁵ Complete quote: "There are only two kinds of people in the end: those who say to God, "Thy will be done," and those to whom God says, in the end, "Thy will be done." All that are in Hell, choose it. Without that self-choice, there could be no Hell. No soul that seriously and constantly desires joy will ever miss it. Those who seek find. Those who knock it is opened." Source: C.S. Lewis, "The Great Divorce."

⁶⁶ Exodus 33:14-19.

⁶⁷ Source: http://benwitherington.blogspot.com/2007/11/for-god-so-loved-himself-is-god.html (accessed 06.24.16).

⁶⁸ Double Predestination is sometimes defined this way. From all eternity, God decrees, some to sin and damnation *(destinare ad peccatum)* and actively intervenes to work sin in their lives, bringing them to damnation by divine initiative. In the case of the elect, regeneration is the monergistic work of God. In the case of the reprobate, sin and degeneration are the monergistic work of God.

Source: http://www.ligonier.org/learn/articles/double-predestination/ (accessed 06.23.16).

⁶⁹ John Calvin said: *"We call predestination God's eternal decree, which He compacted with Himself, what He willed to become of each man. For all are not created in equal condition; rather, eternal life is foreordained for some, eternal damnation for others."* Source: Institutes of the Christian Religion 3.21.5; Calvin 1960:926.

⁷⁰ FAULTY APPLICATION OF SCRIPTURE: "One exegetical fault of Calvinism is its tendency to take specific applications of Scripture and make them universal. For example, Isaiah says, "Your whole head is injured, your whole heart afflicted. From

the sole of your foot to the top of your head there is no soundness - only wounds..." But the prophet is addressing apostate Israel, not making a theological statement about all men everywhere. The same is true of the reference to "filthy rags" (Isa. 64:6), the "leopard" incapable of changing its spots (Jer. 13:23) and the antediluvians whose hearts were "only evil all the time" (Gen. 6:5). To take these texts out of their specific, contextual application and make them props for Reformed theology is an unworthy hermeneutic. The doctrine of Total Inability is not necessitated by the Scripture. Any tenet that portrays God as exacting impossible demands of His creatures and punishing them for not complying is unreasonable. William Ellery Channing notes: "It will be asked with astonishment, how is it possible that men can hold these doctrines and yet maintain God's goodness and equity? What principles can be more contradictory?" Source for the immediate quote: The Works of William E. Channing, "The Moral Argument Against Calvinism," (Boston: American Unitarian Association), 1889, p. 461.

Source for the entire quote above: http://www.auburn.edu/~allenkc/openhse/calvinism.html#Faulty (accessed 08.21.16).

[71] For more commentary here, see: https://blogs.ancientfaith.com/orthodoxbridge/plucking-the-tulip-1-an-orthodox-critique-of-the-reformed-doctrine-of-predestination/ (accessed 07.19.16).

[72] "The ecumenical creeds confess clearly and consistently the vicarious character and saving purpose of the suffering and death of Jesus, that Jesus suffered and died "for us" and "for our salvation." None of these truly orthodox formulations of the apostolic church faith, however, commit any Christian believer to any particular explanation of either the vicarious character

or the saving efficacy of Jesus' death." Quote from: Atonement, Justice, and Peace: The Message of the Cross and the Mission of Church, by Darrin W. Snyder Belousek. Grand Rapids: William B. Eerdmans Publishing. 2012. Page 99.

[73] Eastern Orthodox icon depicting the Emperor Constantine (center), accompanied by the bishops of the First Council of Nicaea (325), holding the Nicene–Constantinopolitan Creed of 381. Source: Google images.

[74] Donald Fairbairn, Life in the Trinity (An introduction to theology with the help of the Church Fathers). Downers Grove: Illinois. InterVarsity Press. 2009.

[75] Ibid. 4-5.

[76] Ibid. 2.

[77] Ibid. 7.

[78] "The Unity of the Church: A Theological State of the Art and Beyond," by Eddy A. J. G. van der Borght. Brill publishers. Leiden (Netherlands). 2010. Page 319.

[79] Source: http://www.desiringgod.org/articles/what-is-the-doctrine-of-the-trinity (accessed 07.08.16)

[80] Source: http://biblehub.com/greek/1834.htm (accessed 06.14.16).

[81] "Sinless perfection" is a heretical doctrine primarily promoted within a certain strand of Arminianism, and especially found within the Wesleyan tradition. Charles Finney taught it prominently. However, the distinction between Wesleyan and Oberlin (Finney) perfectionism can be simplified,

perhaps oversimplified, by saying that John Wesley emphasized the work of God in the perfecting of a life, whereas Charles Finney gave weight to the ability of man to obey God's law. The Hebrew and Greek words translated "perfect" in the English Bible have the idea of "completeness" rather than "flawlessness." We must be careful at this point, however, to remember that heresy exists on BOTH SIDES of an issue/argument. Balance is always necessary!

In the words of A.J. Gordon (of Boston), "If the doctrine of sinless perfection is a heresy, the doctrine of contentment with sinful imperfection is a greater heresy." Gordon went on to say that "it is not an edifying spectacle to see a Christian worldling throwing stones at a Christian perfectionist." Gordon considered, "The doctrine of 'instantaneous sanctification'…the conception…of a state of sinless perfection into which the believer has been suddenly lifted…deliverance from a sinful nature which has been suddenly eradicated…as dangerously untrue," but he also saw the fallacy of "contentment with sinful imperfection." To Gordon, Christianity was not simply a way to escape the wrath to come, coupled with a system to deal with a life of defeat between conversion and heaven. Rather, Christianity is Good News of deliverance. Salvation is deliverance, and the deliverance from sin is not achieved by ourselves. It is bestowed by the Deliverer.

Source: Dr. Rich Flanders: http://ministry127.com/sermon-preparation-helps/sinless-perfection (assessed 08.01.16).

[82] As adapted from "Life in the Trinity" by Donald Fairbairn. Downers Grove: Illinois. InterVarsity Press. 2009.

[83] Source: Rev. Andrew Demotses (Greek Orthodox Church of America).

FROM PART-TWO:
(*Practical* implications of Divine love):

[84] Source: Google-images (Triskelion element of Gothic architecture). (Accessed 08.21.16)

[85] William Barclay, 1999 The Parables of Jesus. page 9

[86] Parables #1-2-3-4 New cloth, New wine. Lamp on a stand. Wise & foolish builders.

Parables #5-6 Moneylender forgives unequal debts. Lamp on a stand (2nd time).
Parables #7-8 Rich man builds bigger barns. Servants must remain watchful.

Parables #9-10 Wise and foolish servants. Unfruitful fig tree.
Parable #11 Sower of seeds into four types of soil.

Parable #12 Weeds among good plants. "Kingdom of Heaven".

Parables #13-15 Growing seed. Mustard seed. Yeast. "Kingdom of Heaven".

Parables #16-19 Hidden treasure. Pearl. Fishing net. Owner of a house. "Kingdom of Heaven".

Parables #20-21 Lost sheep. The sheep, gate, and shepherd.

Parables #22-23 Master and his servant. Unmerciful servant.

Parables #24-25 Good Samaritan. Friend in need.

Parables #26-27 Lowest seat at the feast. Invitation to a great banquet.

Parable #28 Cost of discipleship.

Parables #29-30 Lost sheep (sheep as sinners). Lost coin.
Parable #31 Lost (prodigal) son.
Parable #32 Shrewd manager.

Parable #33 Rich man and Lazarus.
Parable #34 Workers in the vineyard, early and late.

Parables #35-36 Persistent widow and crooked judge. Praying: Pharisee and tax collector.

Parable #37 King's servants given minas.

Parables #38-39 Two sons, one obeys, one does not. Wicked tenants.
Parable #40 Invitation to a wedding banquet.

Parables #41-42 Signs from a fig tree. Wise and foolish servants.

Parables #43-44 Wise and foolish virgins. Servants must remain watchful.

Parable #45 Three servants given talents.

Parable #46 Sheep and goats will be separated.

[87] Source: http://www.orthodoxcatechismproject.org/ (accessed 07.19.16).

[88] Adapted quote from: http://www.christiancentury.org/article/2014-08/parable-and-its-baggage (accessed 07.19.16).

[89] Adapted quote from: http://www.jesuswalk.com/lessons/15_11-24.htm (accessed 07.19.16).

[90] "Divided his property" meant an early distribution of the estate. This normally meant that the father continued to receive the benefits of the estate as long as he lived. This is why the father could "kill the fatted calf" without asking the older son who owned it. In other words, the younger son didn't just receive surplus property; it was part of the father's source of income. The word for property is "bios," meaning "the resources which one has as a means of living" (Source: J. Louw and E. Nida, Greek-English Lexicon of the New Testament, volume 1, page 560, 57.18).

[91] Source: http://www.patheos.com/blogs/christiancrier/2014/04/22/parable-of-the-prodigal-son-summary-meaning-and-commentary/ (accessed 08.01.16).

[92] Source: "The Christian Doctrine of God, One Being Three Persons" by Thomas F. Torrance. Also, see: Incarnation: The Person and Life of Christ, edited by Robert T. Walker, page xxxi (introduction).

[93] St. Symeon the New Theologian, from Galatia (949-1022 AD). Source of quote: http://theodorakis.net/orthodoxquotescomplete.html (accessed 07.19.16).

[94] St. Maximus the Confessor. Died 662 AD. Maximus is venerated in both Eastern and Western Christianity. He was eventually persecuted for his Christological positions. Following a trial, his tongue and right hand were mutilated. He

was then exiled and died on August 13, 662 in Georgia (to the north of Russia).

[95] The Christian Doctrine of God: One Being Three Persons, by Thomas Forsyth Torrance. T & T Clark, Edinburgh. 1996. Page 206.

[96] Ἐν ἀρχῇ ἦν ὁ Λόγος, καὶ ὁ Λόγος ἦν πρὸς τὸν Θεόν, καὶ Θεὸς ἦν ὁ Λόγος. (The Greek translation of John 1:1).

[97] https://afkimel.wordpress.com/2014/03/06/thinking-trinity-no-god-behind-the-back-of-jesus/ (accessed 06.13.16).

[98] *homoousion* - a theological doctrine holding that Christ is <u>of one substance with God</u>. This is in contradistinction with *homoiousia* – which teaches similarity (of similar substance with God) but not identity in essence or substance (not essential likeness). Here we can see just how important (a world of difference) one Greek "iota" makes!

[99] The First ecumenical council was the Council of Nicaea which was a council of Christian bishops convened in the Bithynian city of Nicaea by the Roman Emperor Constantine I in AD 325 in order to attain consensus in the global church through an assembly representing all of Christendom. Although previous councils, including the first Church council (the Council of Jerusalem – Acts 15) had met before to settle matters of dispute. The main accomplishment of this council was to settle the Christological issue of the nature of the Son of God and his relationship to God the Father.

[100] Source: http://www.recus.org/creeds.html (accessed 06.13.16).

[101] Source: "Religion Facts, four of the five Protestant denominations studied agree with the Nicene Creed and the fifth may as well, they just don't do creeds in general". (Accessed October 29, 2014). "Christianity Today reports on a study that shows most evangelicals believe the basic Nicene formulation". (Accessed October 29, 2014).

[102] Source: "Nicene Creed". Encyclopedia Britannica. (Accessed June 16, 2013).

[103] This is a picture of the oldest extant manuscript of the Nicene Creed, dated to the 5th Century

[104] Source: https://afkimel.wordpress.com/2014/03/06/thinking-trinity-no-god-behind-the-back-of-jesus/ (accessed 07.31.16).

[105] George D. Daragas, editor: "The Eternal Son" in T.F. Torrance. The Incarnation: Ecumenical Studies in the Nicene-Constantinopolitan Creed A.D. 381. The Handsel Press. 1981. Reprint: Wipf & Stock. Pages 29-30.

[106] T.F. Torrance (1993:247, 248). http://martinmdavis.blogspot.com/2011/04/tf-torrance-atonement-pt-8.html (accessed 06.06.16).

[107] T. F. Torrance, "The Mediation of Christ," 48-9.

[108] What Saint Paul really said, N.T. Wright. Grand Rapids, MI: Wm. B. Eerdmans Pub. Co., 1997. Pages 132-133.

[109] Source: St. Augustine, Enchiridion, viii.

[110] Source: St. Thomas Aquinas. Summa Theologica "III, 1, 3, ad 3"

[111] Adapted from: Victor Haines: Victor Yelverton. "The Felix Culpa". Washington, D.C. University Press of America. 1982.

[112] Source: https://www.amazon.com/Sinners-Hands-Angry-Jonathan-Edwards/dp/0875522335 (accessed 06.13.16).

[113] http://www.biblebb.com/files/edwards/charity1.htm (accessed 06.13.16).

[114] http://www.biblebb.com/files/edwards/charity1.htm (accessed 06.13.16).

[115] Comments by Dylan Pahman: "Grace and Wrath in the Orthodox Tradition." Source: Ancient Faith Blog. https://blogs.ancientfaith.com/orthodoxyandheterodoxy/2015/02/10/grace-wrath-orthodox-tradition/ (accessed 07.19.16).

[116] Source: https://blogs.ancientfaith.com/orthodoxyandheterodoxy/2015/02/10/grace-wrath-orthodox-tradition/ (accessed 07.19.16).

[117] Source: https://blogs.ancientfaith.com. Ibid.

[118] Commentary lifted and adapted from "Ancient Faith Blog." Ibid. https://blogs.ancientfaith.com/orthodoxyandheterodoxy/2015/02/10/grace-wrath-orthodox-tradition/ (accessed 07.19.16).

[119] Letter to Diognetus 7.4; Richardson 1970:219.

[120] Ware, Kallistos (Timothy). The Orthodox Church. 1963. Edition, 1986. London: Penguin Books. Page 76.

[121] http://www.pravmir.com/the-original-christian-gospel/ (accessed 06.13.16).

[122] http://www.antiochian.org/sinners-hands-angry-or-gentle-god (accessed 06.13.16).

[123] Source: http://www.pravmir.com/the-original-christian-gospel/ (accessed 06.13.16).

[124] Source: Beason Commentary. http://biblehub.com/commentaries/luke/15-20.htm (accessed 07.19.16).

[125] Source: Barnes Notes on the Bible. http://biblehub.com/commentaries/luke/15-20.htm (accessed 07.19.16).

[126] Source: https://e-watchman.com/beware-leaven-pharisees/ (accessed 07.28.16).

[127] I believe this is the standard Siddur given out to Jewish young men on their Bar-Mitzvah.

[128] http://lyrics.wikia.com/wiki/Don_Moen:Think_About_His_Love (accessed 06.06.16).

[129] http://biblehub.com/greek/4697.htm (accessed 06.24.16).

[130] http://www.azlyrics.com/lyrics/christomlin/goodgoodfather.html (accessed 06.06.16).

[131] The Qur'an, Surah 23:102, John 1:1-14-103, 5:9. http://www.exploregod.com/what-makes-christianity-different-from-other-religions (accessed 06.06.16).

¹³² "The Last Judgment" as painted by Michelangelo in the high Middle Ages. In the public domain.

¹³³ In the interest of fairness, there is much truth in Dante's depictions in other portions of his writings (although left unmentioned in this text). The fact is that C.S. Lewis, as a professor of medieval literature at Oxford, was greatly influenced by the writings of Dante' – both agreeing and disagreeing with his characterizations.

¹³⁴ Source of this extended quote: http://blog.cslewis.com/heaven-and-hell-as-idea-and-image-in-c-s-lewis/ (accessed 06.24.16).

¹³⁵ Source: Louis Berkhof, Systematic Theology (Grand Rapids: WM. B. Eerdmans Publishing Co, 1939), 84.

¹³⁶ Ibid. Berkhof, 85.

¹³⁷ Source: Brian C. Stiller. Preaching Parables to Postmoderns. Fortress Resources for Preaching). 2005. Pages 111-112. by Brian C. Stiller

¹³⁸ Source: https://bible.org/article/doctrine-rewards-judgment-seat-bema-christ (accessed 07.19.16).

¹³⁹ William Tyndale, quoted in Iain H. Murray, Evangelicalism Divided (Edinburgh, 2000), p. 1.

¹⁴⁰ Source: https://bible.org/question/what-does-greek-word-tetelestai-mean (accessed 07.19.16).

¹⁴¹ Source: http://www.lighthouselibrary.com/a-wonderful-word/ (accessed 06.24.16).

[142] This definition is according to J.B. Torrance, as quoted: http://thesurprisinggodblog.gci.org/2014/01/what-about-repentance.html (accessed 06.24.16).

[143] Just to clarify this statement – in reality, there is no new thing under the sun (Ecclesiastes). All new heresy is merely old heresy clothed in modern garb.

[144] An antinomian is one who takes the principle of salvation by faith and divine grace to the point of asserting that the saved are not bound to follow the Law of Moses. The term antinomianism emerged soon after the Protestant Reformation (c.1517) and has historically been used as a pejorative against Christian thinkers or sects who carried their belief in *justification by faith* farther than was customary. (Source: Encyclopedia Britannica).

[145] Source: https://bible.org/question/what-are-greek-and-hebrew-words-%E2%80%9Cconfess%E2%80%9D (accessed 07.19.16).

[146] Source: "Expositions of Holy Scripture — Alexander Maclaren" http://biblehub.com/library/maclaren/expositions_of_holy_scripture_e/gifts_to_the_prodigal.htm (accessed 06.13.16).

[147] Source: http://www.gospelresearch.org/ProdigalSon.html (accessed 06.24.16).

[148] Internet article"The Way of Agape: Why Is God's Love So Important?" by Nancy Missler.

Source: https://www.khouse.org/articles/1999/227/print/ (accessed 12.10.16).

[149] Source of extended quote in the last section. Nancy Missler. https://www.khouse.org/articles/1999/227/print/ (accessed 12.10.16).

KNOWING THE FATHER'S HEART

KNOWING THE FATHER'S HEART

KNOWING THE FATHER'S HEART

KNOWING THE FATHER'S HEART